Small By Design

ADVANCED PRAISE

"If you're an entrepreneur with big ideas and a compelling purpose, this brilliant, heartfelt book will help you create a life of abundance and meaningful impact while staying small, by design."

—**Joey Reiman**, Founder of BCG BrightHouse,
Co-Founder and Chairman to Brand New World Studios

"In a world that celebrates big, Feldman lays out a refreshing and necessary argument for why we should consider small, as well as the merits and positive outcomes that result from this shift. This is well worth a read if you're curious about how to make small the shift that creates big results for you!"

—**Darrah Brustein**, hybrid business strategist and life coach

"In his inspiring and masterfully written book, Small by Design, David Feldman guides us to run a successful business with humanity while staying true to ourselves. Small by Design is a powerful playbook that empowers entrepreneurs to live a more satisfying life, connect authentically with people, and develop lasting relationships."

—**Tommy Breedlove**, *Wall Street Journal* and *USA Today* Best Selling Author of the Book *Legendary* and founder of the Legendary Movement.

"Seize this opportunity to design a small company that will embrace and sustain the fullness of who you are and the impact you want to make, while cultivating a culture and community of authentic connection, meaningful engagement, and true belonging. David Feldman's Small by Design will show you how."

—**Perrine Farque**, Author of *Inclusion: The Ultimate Secret for an Organization's Success* and founder of Inspired Human

SMALL
BY DESIGN

The Entrepreneur's Guide for
Growing Big While Staying Small

DAVID FELDMAN

NEW YORK

LONDON • NASHVILLE • MELBOURNE • VANCOUVER

Small By Design

The Entrepreneur's Guide For Growing Big While Staying Small

Published in New York, New York, by Morgan James Publishing. Morgan James is a trademark of Morgan James, LLC. www.MorganJamesPublishing.com

Proudly distributed by Ingram Publisher Services.

A **FREE** ebook edition is available for you or a friend with the purchase of this print book.

CLEARLY SIGN YOUR NAME ABOVE

Instructions to claim your free ebook edition:
1. Visit MorganJamesBOGO.com
2. Sign your name CLEARLY in the space above
3. Complete the form and submit a photo of this entire page
4. You or your friend can download the ebook to your preferred device

ISBN 9781631958854 paperback
ISBN 9781631958861 ebook
Library of Congress Control Number:
2022931057

Cover Design by:
Andra Florea

Interior Design by:
Christopher Kirk
www.GFSstudio.com

Morgan James is a proud partner of Habitat for Humanity Peninsula and Greater Williamsburg. Partners in building since 2006.

Get involved today! Visit MorganJamesPublishing.com/giving-back

DEDICATIONS

For my wife, Alisa, for being the calming force behind my relentless energy.
For my daughter, Tali, who inspires me every day to be a better person.

For my dad, Greg, for lighting and kindling my entrepreneurial fire. For my mom, Helen, for always believing in me. For my sisters, Emily and Michelle, for being the iron that sharpens my iron.

TABLE OF CONTENTS

FOREWORD

About 30 years ago, when I was a young man, I started an ad agency. There were two things notable about the company I had started. The first was that within a year of launching we were doing work with major global brands including AT&T, CNN, Turner Classic Movies, and The Coca-Cola Company.

The second was that I was obsessed with making our firm appear larger than it was. This obsession was driven by a critical misunderstanding that I had—I thought clients were hiring us for our size and scope. But I was wrong about that.

This obsession ultimately resulted in the demise of my company. We were never really profitable, and when the dot com bubble burst, so did my hopes and dreams.

About 20 years later, I met a bright, young executive who was running a successful start-up. His name was David Feldman, and he's the author of the book you have in your hands right now.

To my great surprise, David was able to create amazing work for his clients while also generating a healthy profit.

Over breakfast one day, I asked him how he was able to do such terrific work while also being able to bring home a nice, big profit-sharing check at the end of every year.

"I've realized," he told me, "that clients don't care about your number of employees, or how big your office space is, or how fancy your conference room is. What they're interested in is results. At the end of the day, that's what they hire you for."

David went on to describe more about his business philosophy. He explained that his business was small by design. He had structured his company so that it could scale up when things were busy, and it could scale down when things slowed down. David's structure also allowed him to bring specialized teams to bear on the clients' problems. If he had a client who needed him to create a "blue widget," he didn't use a "green widget" expert simply because they were a full-time employee. Instead, he could hire a blue widget expert specifically for that project.

The results were that he was able to do great work for his clients that generated terrific results, all while making a healthy profit.

The good news about David's experience is that he's put what he knows about business in this amazing book. I wish I had this book in my hands 20 years ago—if I had, I might be writing this from my private island in the Caribbean. (Side Note: I'm writing it from my lake house, so I'm not exactly complaining. But still … you get my point.)

So … here's what to do with this book. Read it, absorb it, and, most importantly, put it into action. There are plenty of amazing techniques that you can put into use right away. And there are a ton of great stories about how David, and many other small by design businesses, put these techniques to work. In the end, you'll learn from both of our experiences—mine, running an unprofitable business that was focused on appearance; and David's, running a profitable business that was focused on results.

With all that said—go forth and prosper.

Jamie Turner
Author, Speaker, and CEO

Preface:

PLAYING EXTRA LARGE
FOR PIZZA MONEY

Pretending To Be Big

was three years into running a very, very small agency: one com-
posed of me, a designer, and one developer. We were making it all
work from a co-work space, or at home on our couches.

Under the limitations of running a small business, I was trying to
make an impact despite miniscule budgets. For every contract I won,
I had to convince another client to take a leap of faith on a $10,000
project. Often they'd try to haggle that amount down to $8,000.

My clients were mostly small businesses, just like mine, with tight
budgets and lean staffs. I usually worked directly with owner-opera-
tors—never with a marketing department, and never with collaborat-

ing vendors. I handled all the ideas, management and strategy, then communicated those to my very small team.

If you've ever worked on a contract like that, you know how it gets stressful for all the wrong reasons: justifying every hour and confronting owner biases, instead of figuring out how to make the biggest impact on a client's business.

Financially strained and energetically drained, I knew I needed to win that first big project: one with a real budget and meaningful collaboration. I needed the resources to bring on a few more people, so I could dream big and deliver greater value.

I was at a crossroads in my career. My present course wasn't sustainable. Something had to shift, and soon.

A Classroom Exercise Becomes a Real World Opportunity

While juggling all this, I was also guest-lecturing at Emory University's Goizueta Business School, where I'd earned my own business degree.

Professor Reshma Shah had invited me to speak to the students in her annual Marketing and Consulting Practicum, on the topic of building a story for a brand. Each year, the class took on a real-world marketing challenge, usually for a client corporation with headquarters in Atlanta.

That semester, the client of focus was Mellow Mushroom. For readers in the Southeast United States, Mellow Mushroom's 300 high-end pizza restaurants may already be a familiar dining experience. Established in 1974, the chain owns its hippie roots with an unapologetically groovy brand that includes psychedelic design and menu offerings such as Kosmic Karma pizzas and Magic Mushroom soup. In-store artwork goes all in on the trippy vibe.

In preparing to give my talk, I read Professor Shah's client brief for Mellow Mushroom, noting with interest that she had a direct connection to their marketing department.

I also took a look at Mellow Mushroom's website and was surprised by what I saw. Here was a big company built on a unique brand identity. But their web presence didn't reflect that. From their language and story to their design and interactive experience—there was a big disconnect between their in-store and online experiences. Swap out the logo, and the website could have been for any generic pizza chain.

I gave my lecture and talked with the students. Afterward, Professor Shah took me out to lunch. I shared with her my assessment of the Mellow Mushroom web experience, and, with some trepidation asked, "What would I have to do to get a meeting with them?"

"Oh, sure, I'll set it up," she replied.

And suddenly a new opportunity was on my doorstep.

A Meeting with Mellow Mushroom

It was June 19, 2015. I know because I saved a screenshot of the email thread. Professor Shah introduced me to a marketing manager at Mellow Mushroom who quickly replied, "We'd like to meet you."

It was a surreal moment for me, not only because of this potential new opportunity, but because of the cosmic resonance.

It just so happened that while I was speaking at Emory and managing my own business, I was also teaching a twice-weekly high school marketing class at a local private school. I had an exercise I gave the students each semester:

"Imagine you have a brand that you love. You love who they are, but you don't love their website. Then you get an email saying you get to meet with the person in charge of that brand. How do you tell them that they need a new site?"

I always enjoyed hearing the students' ideas. And I regularly shared with them what I would do if it ever happened to me.

But now it was happening to me. I was in it, and I knew how I was going to approach it, because I had been teaching my students how to do it all along.

A few weeks later, I was in a room with Mellow Mushroom's marketing director, their head of digital, and one of their field marketing managers.

I told them that they needed a new website just to stay competitive, but that I also had ideas that could unlock new growth potential. They immediately agreed, knowing they needed a new site.

The director of digital said, "I really need to find time to put an RFP together for this." Sensing an opportunity, I offered to outline it for him, and he gladly accepted my offer.

A Too Small Proposal

Within a week, I sent the RFP outline. I told the director that, if he ended up sending it out, I'd love to be considered. Two weeks later, he sent me an RFP that looked very much like the outline I'd provided. And I thought, "Well, here we go!"

Energized, I spent days working on nothing but this proposal. I wanted it so bad. I'd take long walks just imagining all I could do for Mellow Mushroom with an ample budget. The impact I could have on their business. The value I could deliver.

I also asked if I could speak with a couple of Mellow Mushroom's vendors. SinglePlatform, for example, which maintained their online menus. And MomentFeed, which they used for proximity search marketing. I wanted to understand how they interfaced with the website so I could scope a plan for optimized integration, including how the new site would weave existing systems into a seamless brand experience for customers, with an efficient backend for the business.

That due diligence seemed obvious to me at the time, but it turns out I was the only agency to request it. Without knowing it, even before I'd presented my proposal, I'd shown Mellow Mushroom how well versed I was becoming in their business. They could already see that I cared.

Unsure how to price the project, I reached out to a friend of mine who worked at a much larger agency, asking him for advice. I thought he was crazy when he threw out $200,000 as an estimate. I thought it was more like a $30,000 project, still more than twice the size of anything I'd ever taken on before. I eventually talked myself into asking for $70,000—an insane amount of money for me at the time.

When I finished writing the proposal, I printed it all out on high quality 11x17 paper: big, chunky, and heavy, so no one could overlook it. It was filled with my ideas, many of them already very specific and deeply aligned with their business challenges and opportunities.

I then asked to present the proposal, in-person. Again, this seemed to me an obvious thing to do, but again I was the only agency to do so. All the others simply emailed their materials.

Two days after my personal presentation, which I thought went well, I received an email from Mellow Mushroom's director of digital. "Hey, our scope may not have been too clear," he wrote. "You only came in at $70,000."

In retrospect, it's so funny to me. Clearly they had looked at all the work I had done to understand their business and make this detailed proposal. In their minds, a budget of "only" $70,000 meant there had been some mistake.

I played it cool. Went along with the idea that I'd misunderstood a part of the scope. Then I spent a few days figuring out more bells

and whistles I could add to the project to deliver $35,000 more value
—a 50% increase to the budget, which I resubmitted.

The bigger budget reassured them. Apparently quoting over $100,000
made my agency one that could play at the Mellow Mushroom level.

Orchestrating My Office

The next email from Mellow Mushroom came while I was in a weekly
meeting for a nonprofit I was a part of. (Yes, I was checking my email
during a meeting.)

"Hey David. We're thinking that we're going to move forward
with you. We just want to come by and see your office."

When that meeting was over, I went outside and just started
crying. "This is it," I thought. I knew it had to be the best work we
had ever done, by far. And if we delivered, we would forever be in a
new echelon.

But about that office visit…

At the time, my designer and I worked from a low-budget
co-working space, and our developer worked remotely. To say we had
an "office" was a stretch. Moreover, the people who ran the space were
between cleaning services, and it showed. "Business as usual" would
mean Mellow Mushroom arrived to see just me and one other guy,
hanging out with our laptops in a bit of a dump. I knew this meant I
might lose the opportunity.

So I reached out to every local contractor I had ever worked with.
I told them about the Mellow Mushroom proposal, that they'd all get
work on the project if I closed the deal, and that the budget would
allow me to pay them all well. And then I asked them to come work
in my "office" on the day Mellow Mushroom wanted to visit.

I also grabbed a bunch of cleaning supplies and personally cleaned
up the entire building—both floors—so everything looked immaculate.

On the day the digital director was scheduled to arrive, I had nine people present: me, my designer, six contractors, and my high school intern from the marketing class I taught. Another guy—a marketing consultant in his 40s—also used the co-work space and was there that day. Though he didn't work for me, he looked the part.

Everyone brought their laptops and other office supplies to put on their desks. Some included pictures of their family or pets. They set up their stations and then got going on whatever work they had for the day.

When the digital director arrived, he came upstairs and stopped in his tracks. "Oh, cool office," he said. He took a picture with his phone. "Well, this is kind of awkward. Now what do we do?"

I knew then I had the contract, but I offered to introduce him to everyone. We went around, meeting everyone individually, with me telling him about some of the projects each person had handled.

During the tour, one of the contractors—entirely on his own improvised initiative—said, "David, I'm going for coffee. Can I get you two some?"

Needless to say, we got the job.

"But Can He Do the Job?"

There's a recurring line in the Tom Hanks film[1] "Joe Versus the Volcano," a refrain in a one-sided sales call delivered by actor Dan Hedaya: "I know he can get the job but can he DO the job?"

With Mellow Mushroom, the question resounded. There was no doubt they liked me, my agency, and my ideas. They had even told me that they knew they would be taking a risk if they went with a small agency like mine, but they believed that risk would be rewarded, thanks to my extensive research. The depth of my understanding of

---

1 Famously, the star of "Big." Coincidence? I don't think so.

their business. The detail in my proposal. And how I'd shown we had the understanding and expertise to deliver.

But as stewards of a major brand and a major budget (for me at least), the people at Mellow Mushroom still worried whether I could get the job done. My momentarily clean, full, vibrant office hadn't put that to rest.

It took me a while, but eventually I understood it wasn't the size of my agency that worried them. Instead they were concerned we couldn't be relied upon.

Not that those two things aren't related. Worries about an agency's size and its reliability do often go hand in hand. But ultimately, in situations like this, it's likely not really size that anyone's worried about. Instead it's whether you can execute on your big ideas.

Clients are concerned that you don't have the capacity to take on a big job like theirs. That your business isn't stable, and you might not keep your doors open long enough to complete the work.

That worry shadowed us until we finished the Mellow Mushroom project.

Mellow Mushroom's New Groove

When we completed and launched Mellow Mushroom's new site, everyone was thrilled. "We've got the best restaurant site out there," they said.

And I'd thrown everything into it: something a larger, more established agency would never have done. But we were small, young, eager, and just so excited to be working on this big, bold project with all the budget we needed to do it right.

As a result, the site was fantastic—true to the brand and experience I already loved. Groovy, but modern. Playful, yet intuitive. Eclectic and still cohesive. And with built-in metrics, it led to a measurable increase in loyalty club joins and online order sales.

Four years later, as I write this, the site is still live. I know they'll replace it one day, but it still feels fresh and true to who they are. It still pushes the envelope of website artistry and interactivity. Even the current creative leadership at Mellow Mushroom still loves it. (As is common in the field, many of those I worked with on this project have since moved on to other brands.) I had drinks with the creative director a while back, and I told her what we billed for the site. She almost spit out her drink, thinking it was hilarious how little we had charged, though I have no regrets. At the time, that price covered all our overhead and more for a year, and it vaulted us into a whole new league of clients.

Recently, a potential client reached out to me, wanting a restaurant branding project. He told me that his sister had researched all the best restaurant websites, and had found the Mellow Mushroom site. She told her brother they needed the agency that had built that site, so they tracked down my team. Now we're finalizing a contract with them. Not once have they asked to come see my office. They don't care how small we are.

Magic Mushroom Musings

Looking back on the project through which my agency transcended forever to a higher plane, I can see some naive mistakes that I made, choices I would change if I had the chance. I can also see what I instinctually did right in the moment, even if I didn't understand why.

As is so often the case with our learning and growth, I wish I knew back then what I know now. But since I can't go back in time to share what I learned with my younger self, I've decided instead to share it all with you.

I believe I won the contract with Mellow Mushroom because I understood that better ideas mattered more than a bigger office space or payroll.

I started out with a critical observation: there was a jarring disconnect between Mellow Mushroom's beloved in-store brand and their online experience. And I came to them with a clear vision of how we could translate their groovy vibe to a modern web experience.

I also did my homework. I studied their business and learned about the company. I interviewed their vendors and presented a creative vision that was more than simply a cool brand design that might win us some awards. Instead, I grounded my ideas in their business growth, both explaining and implementing metrics to measure how it would generate new revenue while streamlining operations.

Ultimately, the strength of my ideas won me the contract. And none of what I did to develop those ideas required my company to be large. Researching, interviewing, thinking, thinking some more… a solo consultant has just as much access to these tools as a 500-person agency. And if all that thinking yields better ideas, plenty of potential clients will choose the agency with the best ideas over the one with more people at more desks. (You don't want to work with the ones who won't.)

I'm honored that, while feeling they were taking a risk with me, Mellow Mushroom chose to take that risk. It speaks volumes about who they are. But I wish I had done more to take that worry off the table even before it materialized. Instead of thinking, "We're taking a risk," I wish I had inspired them to think, "This agency has great ideas, and, because they're small, they are really going to care about and prioritize this project."

As a result, I do things differently today.

I demonstrate from the beginning that a small company like mine can deliver more value and greater impact, not in spite of being small but because we were small, by design.

For all of you who are starting or already running a small business, I want to help you do that too. I want to help you celebrate being small and leverage that smallness as an opportunity for enormous victories.

That's what this book is all about.

Introduction:

THE DAWNING AGE OF SMALL

A Large Business is Like a Narrowing Corridor

When I graduated with a B.A. in business from Emory University's Goizueta Business School in 2008, no one in my class knew we were about to go through the Great Recession. With degrees in hand from an internationally respected business program, we expected to easily find open doors to opportunity, with the promise of a steady climb up our chosen corporate ladders.

I confirmed that expectation by being lucky enough to get a good job right out of school, at JWT, an international marketing and communications firm. It was, by all appearances, exactly the right way to begin a solid and successful career in corporate marketing. Even more so as the economy started falling apart soon after.

I spent my first six weeks just entering data for one of our client projects. During that time, I realized I didn't know anything about the client, so I looked up their website and read a little about what they did. Though my greater understanding wouldn't have any real impact on the menial work I was doing for them, already I felt the need to find some connection—some meaning in it all.

I knew, of course, that I also had to put in my time, and I was grateful for what I had. By working hard and staying patient, I felt confident I would move up and eventually spend my days on more interesting challenges. No matter what else was happening with the world.

I could get an M.B.A. in a few more years, for example, gaining the received conventional wisdom of how to grow a business and keep rising to the top. I could then get further promoted within JWT, or hired up somewhere else based on my enhanced resume. I could keep working, keep climbing, and progress along this stable corporate ladder of success.

My future was mapped out, and there was a chest of buried treasure awaiting me at the end. I was fortunate, and I knew this. I reminded myself of this. Over and over again. Practiced that gratitude with the same diligence I'd brought to my studies and now my job.

But something still didn't feel right.

I remember looking down the hallway one day at JWT and thinking, "OK, in two years, I'll have this office. In four years, I'll have this office with a window. Maybe in eight to ten years, I'll have that corner office." And though the perks of corporate success did have some appeal (especially in insecure times), I didn't like seeing my future laid out so plainly ahead of me.

I didn't realize it in the moment, but I was already thinking as an entrepreneur of small.

I've never been content when everything is clearly laid out before me. My curiosity has always pulled me toward what I don't yet know, and I've learned I'm happiest when I'm building something new. A clear path forward, defined for me by my large, stable employer? That seemed so limiting and confining.

I shared this story recently with my colleague Neil Bedwell, founding partner of LOCAL (a Change Marketing™ agency) and former Global Group Director for Digital Strategy and Content at The Coca-Cola Company. He had great success working at a large, multinational corporation, but with his new venture he has chosen to stay small.

"A large business is like a narrowing corridor," he told me. "It only allows one person to exit at the end."

Sound claustrophobic? That's how I'd felt too.

If the challenge of becoming that one person fires you up, then large corporate life might be for you. But the reality is that most people get stuck somewhere along that narrowing corridor, managing people in cubicles doing work according to the strategies set by folks in the corner office.

The middle of that hallway can be a dreary place: at a distance from the work that directly impacts the clients, but not in a position to set meaningful strategy for the company. And no matter how far along it you progress, so much of what's possible is predefined by others.

Make no mistake, middle managers are essential for big businesses, but being a part of big business isn't the only way to succeed in a meaningful career.

Still, I was haunted—maybe in the same ways you are now. Could I still make an impact outside these halls? Could I find a more fulfilling path to success and satisfaction?

After considering the discomfort of my very comfortable situation, I thought perhaps I could. Perhaps the world was changing in ways that favored the small. Perhaps I could better serve my clients and myself if I started my own company (with less confining possibilities), and kept it small, by design.

Big Companies Still Own the Widget World

Since the early days of the Industrial Revolution, large companies have been ascendant.

Mass production. Mergers and acquisitions. Multinational corporations. Monopolies.

For more than 250 years, business success has been defined and dominated by the large who get larger, crowding out the world's solitary artisans, solo practitioners, and small businesses.

There was, in the beginning, a certain logic to this growth.

Factories invested in expensive equipment and facilities, then gathered together many people to operate them. Companies coordinated the intricate collaboration of many specialists. Corporations made possible massive efficiencies of scale.

All of this enabled a radical leap forward in the material wealth of the world, its nations, and some of its individuals.

But over time, growth has taken on a self-referential logic of its own: one rooted in size over value. Increasingly, it has become growth for the sake of more growth, and for the power growth gives to overwhelm smaller competitors. As former Chair of the Council of Economic Advisors Austan Goolsbee claimed in the headline for a recent The New York Times editorial, "Big Companies Are Starting to Swallow the World."[2]

---

2   Big Companies Are Starting to Swallow the World," Austan Goolsbee. *The New York Times*. September 30, 2020.

When size became synonymous with success, small became suspect. As the catch phrase said: "Nobody ever got fired for buying IBM." A multinational technology firm with well over a quarter million employees offered security and assurances. A seven-person startup? Sounds risky and uncertain.

This era of big business is certainly not over. Large corporations continue to get larger. Many small companies struggle to survive.

And for companies that rely on streamlined supply chains and economies of scale, bigger may remain better. No small company can (yet) compete with the distribution network of Amazon, the bargaining power of Walmart, or the R&D budget of SpaceX.

Even in industries with more ephemeral outputs, some products and services still require the labor of massive workforces. Disney can't make movies or staff an amusement park without an army of creators or hosts. Microsoft employs thousands of developers to maintain its dominance in office IT solutions.

Where size still does matter, big companies are doing just fine.

There is, however, a rumbling at the roots of the "bigger is better" hegemony.

Amplifying the Impact of Ideas

A funny thing happened on the way to corporate dominion. The very advances enabled by the Industrial Revolution and the Ages of Science and Mass Production ushered in the Digital Age. Those advances at first gave great power to the few, and to the one.

But just as big business seems poised to swallow the world whole, the world itself is changing—in part because of the Digital Age it birthed.

In the economy of ideas, disruptive technologies and macro-economic shifts are now making large companies' historical advantages obsolete. The barriers to small companies are falling, and many now have access to the same high-impact resources as their bigger corporate siblings. For example:

- Online marketplaces give small companies access to international talent.
- Open-source information and on-demand education allow entrepreneurs to acquire new skills and capabilities once held closely by large, legacy companies.
- Remote work and collaboration platforms equip teams to work together efficiently wherever they are, without any office space overhead.

As entrepreneurs learn to leverage these resources, their small companies are delivering value to big clients on a scale once reserved for their much larger competitors. Today, a big staff isn't necessary to deliver a high-value impact. And the advantages of being small by design are winning the day.

Small companies can work more efficiently, utilizing only the truly necessary resources to accomplish their goals.

- In chapter 1, I'll tell you about Perry Construction Management, a small company that oversees major building projects for Fortune 500 clients including Kellogg's, Nestlé, and Starbucks, as well as for the U.S. Federal Government. Founder Ron Perry pairs big ideas with thoughtful leadership to build consensus among many stakeholders. With very small teams, he manages multimillion-dollar construction projects for his clients, completing them on time and on budget.

Small companies can move faster, pivoting overnight to respond to an existential crisis or transformative opportunity.

- As I'll discuss in chapter 2, the small clinical testing network VitaLink played a critical role in responding to the COVID-19 pandemic. Because they had already developed systems that could scale up quickly to large testing needs, they were chosen as one of the testing sites for the Moderna mRNA vaccine. VitaLink's accomplishments were so impressive that the leaders of the U.S. government's Operation Warp Speed paid them a visit.

Small companies can be more flexible in their systems and nimble with their teams.

- In chapter 6, I'll tell you about Carabiner Communications, a PR and communications agency made up almost entirely of senior-level contractors. Without carrying all the overhead of a large, full-time staff, the company can scale up quickly to big opportunities, engaging superstar talent to deliver superior results.

In the B2B economy of ideas, small by design companies are showing they can make an asymmetrical—and prosperous—impact.

Why Large Companies Hire Small

It's not a coincidence that at the same time small companies are delivering big benefits on their own, increasingly, large companies are choosing small when selecting their B2B partners.

As I said in the preface, it turns out larger companies may not actually care about big, fancy offices (or any office), and they don't care about headcount. They just want to know that you can do the job. Furthermore, they're aware of all the changes that let small companies equal the impact of larger competitors—delivered with greater speed, flexibility, and a personal touch.

Consider two examples from leaders in my network...

Zachary Krame (HBO)

Zachary Krame has marketed entertainment brands for more than a decade, first at Adult Swim, then for the last four years at HBO. He's currently the Senior Marketing Manager for HBO and HBO Max original films, series, specials, and live events.

"We use small agencies often," he told me. "In entertainment, the amount of original content we're producing has accelerated. It's an exciting time, but our internal teams are more or less staying the same size, so we rely on agencies quite a bit."

While Krame still turns to larger agencies for HBO's tentpole series, the sheer volume of content to promote means there's plenty of opportunity for smaller agencies too. "When I'm working on a smaller project like a documentary or a comedy special, I look at it as an opportunity to work with a more niche agency that has done good work on something similar to what we're promoting."

He often finds the small agency experience more satisfying too.

"At a big agency," he says, "you have a client person who then relays information to an art director who then relays information to a designer."

This means Krame is several layers removed from the creative people actually doing the work.

Conversely, "At a small agency, you're working directly with the art director or the creative director, even the designer," he says. "It's a much more productive conversation when we have the thought leaders who are living and breathing the creative all in the room together."

Krame also sometimes chooses a smaller agency because he knows that, unlike their larger, more comprehensive competitors, they have particular expertise in exactly what he needs.

"I often work with one husband and wife agency that specializes in designing key art[3]," he says. "If I went to a big agency, I might get eight designers, copywriters, and a creative director on a Zoom call where everyone has a glaze over their eyes. Instead, I get this two-person agency on the phone. They immediately have tons of ideas, and they're just so excited to design key art. It's exactly the right energy for starting off a new project."

The result is more rewarding, project-specific, efficient, and creative work—for Krame and for everyone.

Cliff Corr (Mailchimp)

Cliff Corr is the senior director of customer success at Mailchimp, the marketing, automation & email platform. Mailchimp makes a commitment to small by design companies through both customer and partner relations.

Mailchimp's customers, for instance, are predominantly small businesses, across all industries. They turn to the platform for simple yet sophisticated marketing solutions that don't require the overhead of a traditional marketing department.

"We want to help companies of all sizes grow their business with Mailchimp," says Corr. "We want to empower the underdog to succeed."

This focus on serving small companies is in part an expression of the values of co-founder and CEO Ben Chestnut, who grew up

---

3   You've seen key art everywhere, even if you're not familiar with the term. It's the art and design used consistently throughout all promotions of a film: the movie poster, the social media and print ads, the streaming service menu.

watching his mother run a hair salon out of their kitchen. Similarly, the father of co-founder Dan Kurzius ran a bakery.

But it's also a recognition of a massive opportunity to serve the tens of millions of small businesses in America and the hundreds of millions more throughout the world. In a similar way, the company's partnership program, Mailchimp & Co., pairs small business customers with freelancers and small agencies that can help those customers get the greatest value out of the platform. This opens up massive opportunities and resources for small by design companies, and it benefits Mailchimp too.

"We have service partners all over the world," says Corr. "We're empowering agencies and freelancers to help their clients, and we're giving them the space to be the experts in this field."

These partners now help Mailchimp grow into new specialties and communities without having to recruit, hire, train, retain, and carry the overhead of in-house expertise.

With about 1,200 employees themselves, Mailchimp is certainly not small, and their $12 billion acquisition by Intuit in 2021 makes them part of a roughly 10,000-employee multinational corporation. But their growth strategy still relies heavily on their network of small by design partners. Mailchimp & Co. allows the company to stay lean and nimble while creating mutually beneficial opportunities for an able and ready network of small by design businesses—and provide quality, diverse service to their small customers, too.

The Satisfactions of Small

As I quickly learned at my first job, my priorities weren't aligned with the shape of success offered by a large corporation. I'm not alone in this.

Evolving perspectives on success have been shifting our understanding of a life well lived for some time now. Big business pro-tools may no longer translate into big personal (or even big institutional) triumph.

Rather than simply programming a path to the corner office, everything we do—as Daniel Pink argues in Drive: The Surprising Truth About What Motivates Us—can and should provide us with autonomy, mastery, and purpose. It should all, as a large body of recent research on aging[4] and depression[5] advises, give us opportunities for creativity, social connection, mental stimulation, exercise, and rest. Because that's what will help us all truly prosper.

While some forward-thinking large businesses are attempting to retrofit these qualities into their practices, a small by design company provides these core features right out of the box. It is built from the beginning for meaning.

Small by design success is not a narrowing corridor you spend a few decades walking down. Success is, instead, a story you craft as you go—in collaboration with your team—giving purpose to your work and the legacy you will leave.

And the satisfactions of small are not only for the founders. They flow also to everyone on your team.

When I hired my agency's first project director, she came to me after eight years working at a much bigger agency. When it was time to present the initial website design for a large, national ice cream restaurant brand, I asked her to lead the presentation.

She told me, "David, I've never presented creative to a client before. I've never had the opportunity to be this close to the work."

---

4   See, for example, "Cognitive Health and Older Adults," National Institute on Aging. Retrieved November 29, 2021 from https://www.nia.nih.gov/health/cognitive-health-and-older-adults

5   See, for example, "The Effectiveness of Art Therapy in Reducing Depression in Prison Populations," David Gussak. *International Journal of Offender Therapy and Comparative Criminology*, August 1, 2007.

She was nervous, but I helped her prepare, and then she presented like the pro that she already was. She was thrilled. As the project moved forward, she took real ownership of it and gave the whole of what she had to offer. She was proud of the work she was doing, and it showed.

The client felt it too. She wasn't another disempowered automaton of some bloated bureaucracy, shuffling tickets between clients and creatives, with much lost in translation. Instead, she brought the big picture to the table every time, with the authority of the agency to make decisions in the moment and set them in motion.

A small by design company empowers you and everyone on your team to work with mastery and autonomy, going deep into work that is meaningful to your clients and yourselves.

Another story…

My first creative director came to me straight out of a creative portfolio school. He's brilliant and could have landed a job at a big, elite agency. But then he wouldn't have seen the immediate impact of his work. He told me once about driving down the highway and seeing the billboards for one of our clients, a national brand: how satisfying it was to him to know that he wrote the words on those billboards and directed the design.

He can feel that satisfaction so acutely because there's a very short line from his creative vision to its realization in the world. He can conceive bold ideas that he knows will serve our clients well, confident that they won't be domesticated by internal politics or die by a thousand cuts in committee. What he saw by the highway was the expression of his best ideas.

Clients feel his excitement too, and they're often pleasantly surprised by how easy he is to work with. He doesn't have to calculate compromises or negotiate his way through a morass of management. Instead, he shows up eager to understand each client's needs, then confidently offers up his very best ideas. They have deep, open, and honest conversations, and whatever they agree upon is what we're going to do. Easy.

Showing up fully with engagement and creativity. No bureaucracy, no politics. Real talk that leads to real results. It all allows us to connect with our clients on an authentic, more vulnerable level that serves the work well and makes it more satisfying too.

A company that's not only small but small by design is built to nurture and make the most of human connections: with clients, with employees and contractors, with colleagues, and with community.

It's the same connection I was looking for years ago when I researched JWT's client while I was entering their data.

So much of what small offers is what many have wanted in their work for generations, never finding it in the pursuit of endless growth. We wanted a more meaningful way to apply our skills, make an impact, and succeed.

And today, it's available to us.

That makes small by design more satisfying for the people who work within it, and also for the people they serve

The Small Will Inherit the World

As a new age dawns in the economy of ideas, companies that don't shed the overhead and assumptions of big-company thinking will be left behind by those that figure out how to make the most of being small. You can see it in the stories I've shared with you here, and possibly in your own experiences as well.

If you're creating or building a business that's small by design, you can create big success without taking on the weight of running a large company. You can do it without renting offices. Without payroll stress. Without having to manage a large-scale bureaucracy, becoming further and further distanced from the work that brought you into your field in the first place.

You can stay connected to the work that matters—the work that invigorates you, your teams, and your clients. You can keep almost everything small and lean while working toward large-scale success.

As the necessity of being large fades away, the advantages of being small are poised to win the day. But you don't get those advantages simply by being small. Instead, you have to unlock that power.

We'll spend the rest of this book examining exactly how.

SECTION ONE:

Sustainable by Design

Chapter 1:

TAKE SMALL OFF THE TABLE

From Securing Baghdad to Building the American Dream

Ron Perry is the president and CEO of Perry Construction Management, a small construction management company that oversees major building projects for Fortune 500 clients including Kellogg's, Nestlé, and Starbucks, as well as for the U.S. Federal Government.

As a West Point graduate and veteran of Operation Iraqi Freedom, Perry was no stranger to leading people through complex and challenging missions. Then a divorce led him to leave the military and prioritize raising his children.

It was a new chapter in his life, and he needed a new career. Through a headhunting agency, he was hired to manage construction projects for a large general contractor, even though he knew almost nothing about construction.

"I still don't think I can install an interior door in my own home," he says, "but that's not what I was hired for. The work is actually about understanding people, building teams, building consensus as they work toward a common goal, making decisions, and executing."

His education at West Point and his experiences in Iraq had amply prepared him for the work, even without a construction background. Both his employer and the clients they served were delighted with the quality and efficiency of the projects he led.

Several years later, when Perry started his own, initially solo consultancy, the same abilities helped him convince his clients they could trust his small company with their big-budget construction projects.

Perry never pretended his new company was big. He simply took any concerns about being small off the table.

They're Not Worried You're Too Small, They're Concerned You Aren't Reliable

As I described in the preface about my own first big opportunity, Mellow Mushroom saw early on that my startup agency had great ideas for their brand, no matter our small size. Similarly, Perry speaks eloquently to his clients, sharing his big ideas for managing complex projects, building consensus among stakeholders, and assuring quality and accountability.

For Perry and for myself, convincing clients that we know what we're talking about is easy. No elaborate theatrics to make ourselves look bigger are required, because we do know what we're talking about. Simply sharing our thinking puts any worries about that to rest.

What's harder when you're small is convincing big clients you can execute on your excellent ideas. They want to know if you can do the job. They're concerned you might not be reliable.

Sure, you may be brimming with confidence that you can deliver your enchanting dream into the bright, waking world. But consider the decision from the client's perspective: You're asking them to trust you with a large budget —often millions of dollars in Perry's case, usually hundreds of thousands in mine—to create, improve, or manage something that's critical to their company's stability, growth, and success.

Meanwhile, with large clients, you're almost never personally dealing with the founder or CEO, and, even if you are, they're still answering to a board of directors or other stakeholders. Your point of contact is held accountable for the consequences of the decisions they make, the resources they spend, and the people they trust. Their own careers may rise or fall based on the success of your project.

In the movies, underdogs like you may win big contracts because someone at the company likes your style or has a good feeling about you. But in the real world, decision makers know that their "gut feeling" would be a poor justification should your project go south. They'll need to show they did their due diligence.

If they like your ideas, they want you to succeed. But as responsible leaders, they also need to be convinced you won't fail.

Show Them They Can Count on You

Here's what's not detailed in my triumphant preface story: After my agency won the contract with Mellow Mushroom, I still had to spend a lot of effort and energy, throughout the project engagement, reassuring everyone that we were making timely progress and would deliver on the promise of the pitch I had made.

Pretending to be bigger than we were hadn't solved the core problem. Instead of focusing on spotless baseboards and bustling desks, I should have addressed directly their worries about reliability and taken those off the table.

That's what I do today, in my agency that is bigger but still small, by design. From day one, I say with pride to prospective clients that my agency is small. Then I show them why they can trust us to deliver what we promise.

So how do you do that? Here are several things I wish I had done with Mellow Mushroom, several strategies I now use with every new client.

A Playbook for Putting the Reliability Worry to Rest

Small Business Does Not Mean Small Vision

Big ideas on their own aren't enough to take small off the table, but they are where the client's confidence begins.

With that in mind, don't be a commodity vendor: a provider of goods and services with no investment in the client's strategic direction. Instead, be a partner: interested and engaged in all aspects of your mutual success.

Show them, from the start, that you understand their business, and that you have a bold and clear vision of how you can help their company grow. Articulate that vision early and let it be the lifeblood in all of your conversations: the lens through which you view the project.

For example, the major construction projects Perry Construction Management takes on always have several stakeholders on the leadership team, each with their own priorities. In the initial discovery phase, Perry meets with every stakeholder, including workers on the front lines. "What's important to you," he asks them, "and how can I best represent your interests on this project?"

Their priorities often conflict. The safety manager at a food processing plant wants grit in the floors so workers won't slip, while the food safety manager wants a smooth floor that's easier to clean and sanitize.

Each person involved brings their own role's perspective to defining the project's success. In poorly managed construction projects, that can easily lead to political infighting, which causes delays, budget overruns, and a lower quality end result.

So Perry begins with gaining an understanding of each stakeholder's priorities, then works with the full leadership team to build consensus. He rallies everyone behind an integrated vision of the project's success—one that each player can support.

It's bigger than managing a construction project per the client's specified requirements. Instead, Perry facilitates a clearer, more unified understanding of what everyone needs.

I do the same for my clients all the time. As I'll discuss at length in chapter 2, a network of clinical trials sites once came to my agency wanting to improve their existing online presence. Their website attempted to serve both clinical trial sponsors and participants, but it wasn't doing either particularly well.

After carefully studying their business, we came back with a bigger idea: split the website in two. One site to serve the pharmaceutical companies and scientists. One to serve the participants. We also proposed to integrate several backend tools that would not only simplify management of the two sites, but streamline their back office operations.

We proposed a bigger budget than they had originally anticipated, but it was based on a bolder vision of how a multisite network and a well-integrated digital experience platform could help their business grow while operating more efficiently. The company appreciated our understanding of their business and the broader perspective we had brought to what started out as a straightforward website redesign. They approved the larger spend.

Thinking bigger in this way for your clients doesn't have to cost you more money, but it can certainly raise your project budget!

"When in Charge, Be in Charge"

On any project you take, there will be boundaries to your authority: decisions only your client can make, actions only they can take. But within your areas of action and authority, embrace your responsibility and lead the way.

There are many styles and modes of leadership, and I'm not saying you must issue orders and demand unquestioning obedience. Collaborative leadership is a powerful thing.

But entrepreneurs are not followers. Meek deference and people pleasing will not teach your clients to trust you. However you lead, do so with conviction and all the confidence your expertise deserves.

"When in charge, be in charge," Perry says, quoting a military aphorism. The idea behind it is that, within the bounds of the mission and their commander's intent, military units shouldn't wait for detailed directives. They should take initiative, make decisions, and get the job done.

When Perry starts a new project, he declares his responsibility to everyone involved, including all the company personnel on the floor. "If you see any contractor not doing what they're supposed to be doing, call me," he says. "I personally will handle it."

Don't complain to the company's project manager, he tells them. Don't take it to the construction contractor. Perry Construction Management is managing this project, so bring all your concerns to me.

Not only does this declaration send a strong message about Perry's leadership, it's also a relief to the company project managers, who mostly dread all the complaints they'll get during a typical construction project.

Similarly, my agency's clients come to us because of our expertise in tech-forward brand development and integrated digital experience platforms (DXPs). I don't tell them how they should run their restaurants, universities, performance venues, clinical trial sites, or residential communities. But I confidently take charge of developing and implementing their digital brand strategies.

That's what they hire us for, so I lean into the challenge and lead the way. That's what reliable agencies do.

Invest Early In The Relationship

Do you see a potential client turning into a long-term partnership? Are you particularly interested in winning a project? Do you want to take small off the table right away? Invest early in building and strengthening the relationship. Maybe right when you get the project, or even before you do.

A few examples…

My agency was courting a client who offers high-end luxury cruises around Aruba. The owner happened to mention that he would be staying in his favorite hotel in Aruba the week my proposal was due. So I arranged to have a bottle of champagne and a handwritten letter waiting for him in his hotel room when he arrived. He approved my proposal the same day he received it.

Another time, we signed a franchised client for a website project. Branding wasn't part of the initial deal, but I threw in an initial brand workshop. (I normally charge $10,000 for this service.) This added value built trust early on and encouraged the client to think bigger about what we could do. They've since expanded the scope of our work well beyond their website.

One last example: We signed a famous national restaurant brand based 1,000 miles away from me. The initial project was small, and there was no practical need for any of us to meet in person. No matter. I flew with my leadership team up to their headquarters, and we all went to dinner at their restaurant to meet their C-suite. We've since become their agency of record. We're also building a strong relationship with their chief investor and hope to work with more of their brands.

These early investments build stronger client relationships, just as they do for big businesses. But there's an added benefit when you're small by design. Generosity early signals that you have money to spend. It's a cue that says "stability" while previewing for the client the pleasures of working with your company.

So show them, early, that you aren't pinching pennies. Give them some added value when appropriate. Surprise them with your commitment to the relationship. It will take small off the table!

Lead With Your Values

Just like big ideas, strong core values can have an outsized impact no matter how small you are. If those values are truly held, consistently lived, and aligned with your clients', they can go a long way toward building trust and confidence in your company.

At a small by design company, you have direct and daily access to your company's values, an advantage no large corporation can match. Those values are not the artifacts of some committee or consultancy, perceived dimly and distantly through corporate policies and practices. They're your values. You lead with them. You and your team live and breathe them every day.

"I learned in the Military Academy that there's one thing no one can take from you, and only you can give away," says Perry, "and that's your integrity. It's our first core value and central to my company. There are no circumstances, no dollar amount when we would compromise our integrity on the job site."

This isn't a sales pitch for Perry. It's who he is and how he would run his company no matter how his clients felt about it. That is, after all, how core values work. You don't just say them; you live them, consistently, even if the people around you don't care or don't agree.

However, for the right clients—the ones in alignment with Perry's values, and the only ones he'd want to work with—witnessing that integrity is profoundly reassuring.

"By sharing your core values, by showing people what's important to you as a company," says Perry, "you build trust and stronger relationships."

And when clients truly trust you, small is off the table.

As you might already be thinking, not just any values will do. Your values must be true to you, but they must also be values that inspire trust.

Integrity is a powerful value that shows clients your word is your bond.

I'd add transparency and service to the list.

At my agency, we share everything with our clients: our actual best advice (delivered with kindness), the thinking behind our work… even the ideas that didn't work out, and why. Better to talk it all through openly than to hide in an esoteric aura of abstract infallibility.

It may sometimes feel counterintuitive, but being honest and open even about your mistakes builds trust between you and your clients. It reassures them that you're not hiding anything from them, and it gives you the opportunity to better explain your process and thinking.

Similarly, I refuse to let my ego or the ego of anyone on my team get in the way of serving our clients' best interests. We don't develop brands to win industry awards or other accolades for ourselves. We don't cut corners to squeeze out extra margins. We build brands that work for our clients.

We live the value of service in every decision we make, and clients soon learn to trust that we'll always choose what's best for their success.

That's trust that even—maybe especially —large companies often struggle to earn. But when service is a core value of your small by design business, your clients feel it. And the trust that builds is profoundly reassuring.

Relationships are Everything

When you own a small company, it's easy to get awed by the prospect of "working with Kellogg's," as Perry does, or "working with The Coca-Cola Company," as I have.

But the truth is we don't have relationships with these massive corporations. We have relationships with individual leaders and decision makers who work for these companies. We have relationships with people.

I'll go into some of the finer points of this in chapters 8 and 9, but the critical insight here is that you are an individual building relationships with other individuals. You can do that just as ably as someone who works for a much larger company, maybe better, because small by design clears away so many of the institutional barriers to human connection.

"Success wasn't about me trying to convince a large corporation that I'm good enough to work for them," says Perry. "It distills down to individual relationships you have with people, the people who are actually going to be there with you in the trenches, working on the project. It's those relationships and the trust that you build that really determines the success or failure of the project. Those relationships really are the reasons why I have success today."

Show Them Your Structure and Systems

Client concerns about your reliability come in part from fears that, as a small company, you could be just making it all up as you go along.

Counter that assumption by telling people early about your company structure and systems, and explaining to them how these will support the project's success.

This may feel a little forced at first. Large, established companies don't have to explain their structure and systems in order to win their clients' business. But that's because everyone just assumes they have them. Companies don't get large in the first place if they don't have structure and systems in place. (That's the assumption, at least.) And even if those systems become bloated and burdensome, slowing down the work and becoming a fatiguing frustration for their clients, at least no one thinks that the company is just winging it.

As a small by design company, however, you can't rest on the same assumptions. You're small enough that you could be squeaking by, with each day its own ad hoc adventure.

So you have to show your clients that this is not the case. (I'll talk more in chapter 2 about how to put those systems in place if you don't already have them.)

How do you stay organized? How do you keep projects on track? How will you communicate with the client as the project progresses? Transparency is key.

Perry's 16-person team includes a COO, project directors and managers, a client services manager, and a growing team of construction managers. They have well refined systems for taking on new projects and coordinating their work. Perry shares all of this with clients and prospects: on his website, in sales pitches, and in introducing his clients to his team and how they work.

I'm the director of strategy at my agency. My leadership team also has a creative director, a director of web development, a project manager, an account manager, and an administrative assistant. From the beginning, I explain to new clients each of our roles and responsibilities, and I share with them the systems of how we work together.

Do clients need to know whether you've implemented Asana, Basecamp, or Monday as the platform for your project management? Not really, but telling them what you're using and how you'll use it with them shows that you're thoughtful about your systems. This will help build their confidence in your company, regardless of your size.

For example, my agency promises new clients that we will always answer their questions within one business day. That's not just a pretty promise. As we tell them, we track our response times in our project management software. There's a system in place holding us accountable to our commitments, and that's much more reassuring than a promise alone.

Define Your Process for Deliverables

Deliberate transparency not only puts to rest any client concerns that you're making up your systems as you go. It also shows that you have a well-defined process for deliverables. This reassures clients that you've successfully completed projects like theirs before, and you already know how you'll do the same for them.

So don't just have those processes internally. Define them explicitly for your client, at the beginning of each project and at key points along the way.

Create and share a clear and well-designed document that shows clients what they can expect at every step of the project. What are the milestones and timelines? What are the contingency plans if things don't go as scheduled? As I'll cover in greater depth in chapter 2, clear systems like these are critical if you want to have a big impact. They'll reassure your clients as well.

Once clients understand that there's a detailed process and plan, it's a lot easier for them to trust you'll get it done.

Perry Construction Management shares with all prospects their Strong Foundation Approach. It's on their website and downloadable as a PDF. They write about it on their blog, and Perry talks about it in detail with every potential client.

"It explains our four steps for guaranteeing project success," says Perry.

Notably, execution of the construction plan is step three in the four-step process. "It's more than following the plan," Perry says. He first emphasizes all the discovery and planning that goes into executing a project with success. And the final closeout phase reassures clients there won't be any loose ends.

Introduce Key Team Members

You're small, but not alone.

Whether with employees, contractors, or a hybrid of both, you've assembled a team that lets you scale up to do big work. (I'll talk more about creating a powerful team of contractors in chapter 6.) So introduce key members of your team throughout the proposal process. This can even happen via email: "I'm copying in our creative director.

She'll be overseeing our design team and can answer any questions you may have about design throughout the process." This deepens the client's relationship with your team, and encourages greater trust.

This is also a great opportunity for each team member to start building their own relationship with the client, expressing their enthusiasm and sharing a bit of their well-aligned vision for the project's success.

In the early days, Perry was a one-person show, and earning trust in him was the same as earning trust in the company.

As the business has grown, he has assembled a full team and taken on several additional construction managers who do the work that he alone once did. When the company is trying to win a new contract, it's no longer enough for Perry to earn their trust. Once clients meet key members of his team, they learn to trust the whole company too.

This is my approach precisely. Introduce potential new clients to my key team members. Let them experience firsthand our shared values. Let them see the quality of my team's thinking, and the areas of expertise in which they surpass me. Together, we can do so much more, and clients can see that once they meet everyone involved in their project.

Share Your Thinking and Success

I'll go deeper into this point in chapter 5, but no client will care how small your company is if you establish yourself as a leading authority in your field. Stories of your successes and testimonials from satisfied clients will also go a long way to ease any client concerns.

To establish this authority myself, I write and publish regularly in major outlets of relevance to my clients. I speak solo and on panels at industry events. I guest lecture at Emory University's Goizueta Business School. And, hey look! I even wrote a book!

I also continually share all this content with prospective clients. In addition to reinforcing my clout in the industry, it saves me time. Instead of explaining at length to each new client why we insist on designing for website accessibility, I just send them the article I wrote for Forbes about the business benefits of doing so, followed by the series of articles I wrote for Torque on website accessibility best practices. I might even send a link to the video of me talking on the topic at a WP Engine conference.

Does my small agency know how to design an Americans with Disabilities Act compliant website? Are we looking out for the best interests of our clients when we design a site? No one asks those questions after I share all that content.

I also produce and share strong case studies detailing some of the work my agency has done. Don't worry if you don't have a big client to feature. It's just as useful to go deep on the work you have accomplished with smaller clients. Share before and after metrics that clearly demonstrate your impact. Explain the process that delivered those results.

And of course there's nothing like third-party validation to reassure new clients you'll deliver results. Gather testimonials from every happy client… and anyone else who can speak to the impact your company has. Publish them on your website. Quote them in your proposals. Share them on your social media accounts. Let your potential clients know how happy your previous clients have been.

Go a step further and offer to connect prospective clients with your references. I do this all the time, telling the prospect that a few key references would love to tell them more about their experiences working with my agency. Then I ask, "Can I connect you with them?"

These third-party validations will put your new clients at ease, and maybe even get them thinking about the testimonial they'll give when the project is done.

Sidebar: Fear is a Lack of Knowledge

When I was interviewing Perry for this book, he had a piece of advice that doesn't fit neatly into this chapter, but I wanted to share it with you just the same. I guess you could say it's about taking small off your own personal table.

"Fear is a lack of knowledge," he says.

Risk is inherent to entrepreneurship, but you can't let fear prevent you from taking action.

When he started Perry Construction Management, he didn't have a degree in business. Like many small business owners, he was doing everything himself. He incorporated his company using Legal Zoom. Wrote out his own invoices. Tracked expenses with Excel.

In the early days, he worried he might be audited or shut down. He wasn't intentionally doing anything wrong. There was just so much that he didn't know, and he feared he might make a fatal mistake out of ignorance.

But it turns out, "I didn't have to worry about that," he says. "The government doesn't exist to crush small businesses."

Knowledge is the best cure for that fear.

"Whatever is keeping you from wanting to step out," he says, "write it down, then look for answers."

Perry reached out to friends, including one who is a bookkeeper. He enlisted mentors and sought out advisors. As he learned more, he worried less.

"Instead of worrying about mistakes," he says, "spend that energy focusing on the product or service you're providing and make that the best it can be. You'll get more and more business that way, and as you grow, you can start adding people and processes to guide you better along the way."

Building Up From the Strong Foundation

Perry now has six additional construction managers working for his company. Half have a military background like his. All have the leadership qualities and share the values that are the foundation of the company's success.

"I hire for leadership first, and experience second," says Perry.

His own career in construction management wasn't built on knowing how to install doors or floors. He started from knowing how to bring people together, build consensus around common cause, then lead them to success. From his clients' construction projects to his own team's success, he continues to build up from that strong foundation.

While he's no longer a sole practitioner, his company remains small by design. None of his clients care. Through his leadership, his ideas, his values, and the relationships he has developed, all his clients know that they can count on him to deliver exceptional value. They don't care how many employees he has or how big their offices are. They know he can do the job, and that takes small right off the table.

So what do you do when your efforts to prove you can do the job are so successful that you win a contract much larger than anything you're handled before? I have a story about that for you in chapter 2.

Chapter 2:

THE FOUNDATIONS
OF FLEXIBILITY

Accelerating a COVID-19 Vaccine to Warp Speed

On July 27, 2020, in the depths of the COVID-19 pandemic, the NIH's National Institute of Allergy and Infectious Diseases (NIAID) and biotech company Moderna announced that they had begun phase 3 trials of mRNA-1273, a candidate COVID-19 vaccine.[6] According to CNN, on that day the vaccine or a placebo was given to 1,290 people, of a planned 30,000 volunteers overall.[7]

---

6   "Phase 3 Clinical Trial of Investigational Vaccine for COVID-19 Begins," NIAID press release. July 27, 2020. Retrieved December 1, 2021 at https://www.niaid. nih.gov/news-events/phase-3-clinical-trial-investigational-vaccine-covid-19-begins

7   "Fauci 'satisfied' with enrollment for the first week of Covid-19 vaccine trial," Elizabeth Cohen and Dana Vigue. CNN, August 6, 2020. Retrieved December 1, 2021 at https://www.cnn.com/2020/08/06/health/coronavirus-moderna-volunteers-fauci-satisfied/index.html

Just five weeks earlier, one my agency's longtime clients, VitaLink Research, was selected by Moderna and NIAID to participate in a pivotal clinical trial to test the safety and effectiveness of Moderna's COVID-19 vaccine. VitaLink set an initial, ambitious target of recruiting 400 of the study's 30,000 participants. It was a goal they would end up exceeding by nearly 300%.

VitaLink CEO Steve Clemons immediately contacted me and asked for my agency's help in volunteer recruitment. Everyone would have to move fast. The health and lives of millions of people depended upon it.

But because both VitaLink and my agency had solid foundations that allowed for flexibility, we were ready.

Agility is Not Ad Hoc

Agility is often cited as one of the key advantages that small companies have over their larger competitors.

As Ron Perry, from chapter 1, told me, "It's easier to turn a sailboat than a battleship."

Though this advantage is real, it's not automatic. The work that goes into developing effective agility is often overlooked.

Make no mistake, small companies can be just as slow to adapt as large companies, though usually for different reasons. Massive corporations may be weighed down by their bureaucratic burdens: a problem of having too many systems, or systems that are too rigid. In contrast, small companies are often slowed down by their lack of good systems.

When you're reinventing the same wheel every single day, you're never going to get around to building the rest of the wagon.

Small by design companies know how to strike the right balance between the two extremes. They streamline repeatable processes, continually refining them for greater efficiency. But they're also careful not to crush creativity and innovation under the weight of overengineered infrastructure.

True agility comes from building a platform of processes from which your team can leap and fly.

Designed to Scale at Speed

As I'll discuss at greater length in both chapter 6 and chapter 7, small by design companies sometimes have to scale up rapidly (and often temporarily) to meet the demands of big opportunities.

When you're small by design, this is something you should plan and prepare for. The good news? Scaling at speed is simpler when you're small.

When Moderna approached VitaLink, the company's five testing sites were operated by a barebones staff and a three-person leadership team.

Several years earlier, after buying out a private equity firm that had imposed a top-heavy corporate structure, VitaLink made a conscious decision to restructure. They wanted their fixed operations to be as lean as possible, but with the ability to scale up quickly when opportunities to take on large trials came along.

Obviously, they did not foresee the COVID-19 pandemic in its particulars. However, with two decades of experience running clinical trials, VitaLink understood that public health emergencies of this nature do emerge. Their principal investigators, clinical research coordinators, and site managers all knew, based on previous studies they had conducted, that government agencies and pharmaceutical companies would respond rapidly to such emergencies. Which would create an urgent need for clinical trials at scale.

VitaLink wanted to be ready when such critical needs arose. And fortunately for all of us, they were.

Here's how you too can be ready when big opportunities come your way.

A Playbook for Building the Foundations of Flexibility

Establish the Right Roles and Responsibilities

One of the joys I find in running a small business is the collaborative nature of the work. My account manager weighs in on brand strategy. My virtual assistant has helped improve our project management systems. My web development manager offers ideas on business growth.

There's great value and satisfaction in the fluid boundaries of our roles, but they are still very clearly defined. Each of us knows where our responsibilities begin and end.

Small by design companies need this clarity just as much as large corporations. It's how you ensure that all aspects of a client project are covered and handled well. It helps you avoid competing and conflicting decisions, and manage all aspects of your business effectively and efficiently.

That said, you don't have to copy the corporate org charts of large corporations, or even those of other small companies like your own. Don't add a position just because other companies have it. Instead, consider what roles and responsibilities make the most sense for you and your business.

For instance: Once VitaLink was out from under private equity control, the founders scrapped the C-suite structure, which had weighed them down with top-heavy compensation packages and a CFO-imposed reluctance to invest.

"Most CFOs will try to save their way to the bottom line," says Clemons, "but a CEO should be finding a way to spend in order to grow. We had a CFO who basically controlled everything in the company, so we became known as cheap and cheerful, but then eventually cheap and not so cheerful."

When the slate was newly wiped clean, VitaLink crafted a lean leadership team of Clemons as CEO, Haley Williams as VP of Quality, and Gary Clemons as VP of Operations—all three of them founders of the company and members of the board of directors. Soon after, they added a director of business development. They also had several Principal Investigators (the scientists running the clinical studies), with two of them rounding out the five-person board. But that was it.

This new leadership structure reflected the key elements of success in VitaLink's industry. While not every small by design business needs a VP of Quality, a company running clinical trials lives or dies on its reputation for conducting quality research. Not every small business has operations complex enough to merit a VP of Operations, but running large scale clinical trials certainly does. VitaLink designed their leadership based on exactly what would help them function most effectively.

With their two key pillars of success led by trusted VPs, Clemons as CEO could then focus on growing the business… and on preparing for bigger opportunities to come.

My own agency's reorganization was also a response to the COVID-19 pandemic, a time during which I fully embraced the small by design philosophy I'd been developing since escaping that narrowing corridor.

I run a tech-forward branding agency, but I identify as neither a designer nor a developer. In the solo days of my company, I explored both (and it served me well), but, for the next stage of my agency's growth, I needed the freedom to focus my time on my own areas of greatest strength. Namely, to define our clients' problems and opportunities, identify the best solutions, and bring together the right people and resources to do the job well.

Once that's accomplished, I largely get out of the way and let my creative director, web development manager, and account manager run the show. This frees me up to spend more time on long-term strategy and business growth, as I believe a founder and director of strategy should.

Like VitaLink, when given the opportunity to reorganize, I carefully considered our priorities first. Creative direction and web development are central pillars of the value my agency delivers, and that's now reflected in my agency's new leadership structure. It would be complete overkill for us to have a VP of Operations, because our operations are far too lean to merit it. And our finances certainly aren't complex enough for us to require a CFO.

The point here is that your company's structure should reflect the unique value you provide. Create well defined roles to lead what matters most for your company's success. Then spare yourself the overhead of any additional roles you might implement just because everyone else seems to have one.

Standardize Your Systems

VitaLink began as a loosely woven network of five independent clinical trial sites, collaborating under the name Alliance Biomedical Research (ABR). The idea was for these very small sites to work together to secure clinical trials larger than any of them were equipped to win on their own.

It was a good idea in theory, but the complexity of managing this coalition ended up holding everyone back. Among other challenges, each site had its own systems for regulatory compliance, standard operations, and patient recruitment. No study sponsors wanted to navigate five different systems within ABR—that's why they typically chose larger clinical trial networks instead—but the company struggled to present their patchwork of systems as a unified whole.

When the private equity firm fully merged the five sites into one, cohesive company, a truly unified network became much more productive. And when the founders regained the company's independence, they doubled down on this standardization across the board.

Regulatory startup procedures for clinical research studies are, with good reason, complex and labor-intensive, but they are largely the same for every study: a repeatable process that can readily be systematized.

So as part of their new beginning, VitaLink codified these processes and created a leadership position to manage them. Now that person serves as the single point of regulatory contact across all VitaLink sites, continually refining the process to make it extremely efficient. They're responsible for getting sites up and running quickly when a new study comes along. They also manage ongoing regulatory work that has to be submitted throughout the study in order to stay compliant.

This has all greatly streamlined the process of starting and managing new studies that draw on the combined resources of all VitaLink's sites.

In an effort to even more efficiently unify systems, VitaLink also wrote up standard operating procedures (SOPs) that cover everything from training, to data management, to monitoring visits and even drug storage. Their SOPs include:

- Good Clinical Practice (GCP) Training
- Authority and Delegations of Responsibilities of Research Staff
- Subject Screening and Recruitment
- Informed Consent Process and Documentation
- Eligibility Confirmation
- Source Documentation
- Data Management

- Protocol Deviations
- Adverse Events and Serious Adverse Events Reporting
- Confidentiality of Information
- Drug/Device Storage, Accountability and Management
- Regulatory Document Submission Process (Initial Submissions, Amendments and Continuing Reviews)
- Sample Processing and Shipping Training
- Monitoring Visits
- Sponsor, CRO and Internal Audits
- FDA Audits
- Record Organization and Retention
- Sub-Site Management
- Writing SOPs

(That's right, they even wrote an SOP to standardize writing new SOPs. Amazing.)

Though such an exhaustive list of SOPs would be overkill for most small companies, for VitaLink they are central to the value they deliver: well-run studies that produce high-quality scientific results in full compliance with all regulatory requirements. It's a flexible foundation of operational excellence, streamlined and scalable to take on big opportunities with ease.

Because of all the work VitaLink put into developing and refining these systems, when the Moderna trial—and all the urgency of a global pandemic—came along, they didn't have to invent procedures in the midst of the crisis. This urgent, large-scale trial was what they had already planned for. They were ready to go.

While not every small business will need the plethora of SOPs that VitaLink has developed, every small by design company should identify the processes in their work that are repeatable. Then create standardized systems (documented in an SOP) to manage them for efficiency and reliable results.

Just as it did for VitaLink, a foundation of such systems will streamline your work while preparing you to scale at speed when big opportunities come your way.

Plan for a Pilot Period

While VitaLink's SOPs cover everything that could be standardized, every study's protocols are in some ways unique. So, after planning out how to implement any given trial's requirements, the company also practices internal dry runs of the entire process. They look for bottlenecks, gaps, and anything else that could interfere with a study's safe, accurate, and efficient completion.

Once VitaLink has their processes optimized, they still plan for the first few days of any new study to be light, enrolling fewer patients than the study's daily maximum. This gives VitaLink a real-world pilot period during which to test processes and fully optimize the study, and a strong foundation on which to make significant and scientifically sound contributions to its results.

While the stakes aren't usually as high at my agency or any other small by design business, I see this experimental systems mindset as one that can benefit any organization.

For example, my agency tried out several different project management platforms before settling on the one that suited us best. During the pilot period for each solution we tested, we didn't invest hundreds of hours in configurations or transfer every aspect of every project all at once.

Instead, we played around with each candidate solution, tested it out, and investigated whether it supported the way we work. Only when we knew we had found the right fit did we put in the time to more fully implement the platform. This experiment-and-test approach allows my agency to grow new systems and solutions, while keeping our risks low. We investigate and iterate, then only invest fully in a system once we know it will serve us well.

I even apply this principle to taking on new clients. Often I'll propose an initial, three-month "pilot retainer," during which we get a better sense of how we'll work together. If we need to make adjustments in the scope or terms of the retainer agreement, we can do so without waiting for a year or going through the awkward process of renegotiating a contract. At the end of that initial three months, we usually know enough about each other to transition confidently to a full year retainer.

As you develop your own company's systems, don't be afraid to try something new, but pilot test before you invest too much in implementation. You'll save yourself a lot of wasted resources while exploring what works best for your company.

Streamline Staffing and Training

As a small by design business, you'll never have to hire and train hundreds of employees. (Well, maybe you will, but you'll be headed out the door of the small by design club, with all our best wishes for your large by design success.)

But you will hire people, both employees and contractors, sometimes on a permanent basis and sometimes only for the duration of a project.

So how will you identify the qualities and experience you need in those people? Where will you find them? How will you select them? How will you train them and integrate them into your team? Answering those questions now will save you a great deal later.

VitaLink's most variable staffing need is for clinical research coordinators, nurses, and physician assistants. The company has standardized job descriptions for these roles, and well developed processes for recruiting and hiring. They also have one person in charge of all training, which is standardized across all five sites.

This means VitaLink can recruit and train staff quickly when big studies come along. And when the Moderna trial arrived, they were ready to staff up to the needs of the massive new study.

At my agency, I don't hire people often, and my network of trusted contractors is well established and fairly stable. (I'll talk a lot more about that in chapter 6.) Nonetheless, in preparation for that need whenever it arises, my creative director and I spent days together in conversation, fully articulating our agency's culture, values, and methods.

When I do hire someone new, we hand them the document that emerged from those discussions. They don't have to infer our culture and values from our day-to-day encounters; it's all spelled out for them, greatly accelerating how quickly they can fully integrate into my team.

Was preparing that document a lot of work for an agency that only hires 1 to 2 new people per year? Indeed. Was the upfront work worth it to provide a faster onboarding process for those new hires? Absolutely.

Develop Your Digital Infrastructure

Even though my agency is built on bringing digital acumen to building brands that work, I firmly believe that businesses truly succeed or fail based on the quality of their ideas and the capabilities of their people.

That said, your company's digital infrastructure absolutely can empower or impede the ability of your people to effectively implement your team's best ideas. Technology is not the primary reason your small by design business can compete with larger companies, but it sure does help.

Notice the tasks and processes you find yourself completing repeatedly. Unless they're unique to only your business (and very few are), there's a good chance other people are repeating them too. You could probably hire someone to do that work for you, but there's a good chance some entrepreneur has developed a digital tool to automate it. Whenever you can do so without sacrificing quality, keep your team lean and develop your digital infrastructure instead.

How elaborate a digital infrastructure you need will vary widely depending on the nature of the work your company does. Maybe all you need is a basic website with a contact form, reliable email, and some simple cloud storage for shared documents. Maybe you need something far more complex.

The key is to assess your present needs and anticipate how they will change as you scale up to the demands of bigger opportunities. Implement quality digital infrastructure before those most challenging opportunities come along.

At VitaLink, Clemons knew that any opportunities for large-scale clinical trials would require the company to quickly recruit hundreds or even thousands of participants. But like most clinical trials companies at the time, VitaLink had a single website that attempted to serve all stakeholders: scientists, biotech and pharmaceutical companies, government agencies, and participants.

While the first three audiences had largely overlapping needs, participants generally did not have the scientific sophistication expected by the other audiences, and were also looking for different things altogether.

In my team's work with VitaLink, we concluded that, by trying to serve these very different audiences, the single website wasn't serving either very well, so we recommended creating two separate sites. One would emphasize scientific methodology, biotech ROI, and stream-lined logistics for scientists, biotech companies, and government agencies. The second would be dedicated solely to volunteer recruit-ment and participant communication: consistent with the overall VitaLink brand, but slightly softer and warmer, with simpler language and effortless connection.

It would be a lot of work to build out rapid recruitment capabil-ities that VitaLink didn't currently need, but Clemons was looking ahead to the time when they would. He accepted our recommenda-tions, and we got to work.

When Moderna came calling in June of 2020, the necessary infra-structure was already in place.

Nurture the Relationships You'll Need Before You Need Them

Even in ordinary times, the work of any small by design business (and, really, any business) relies on a lot of good relationships.

You rely on your banker and maybe the print shop down the street. The staff at city services and perhaps the coffee shop down-stairs. A caterer, an ad rep, an office supply store. The company that runs the co-work space that you use as your office. All of these con-nections contribute to your success.

But some of these relationships become suddenly even more important when a big challenge or opportunity comes your way. In such situations, you need trusted partners you can call in with urgency, knowing they'll get the job done, whatever it takes.

These relationships can't be built under the pressure of present need. Nurture them before you need them.

My agency had been VitaLink's branding and marketing partner for several years before the Moderna trial came along. Their market-ing budgets were modest at the time, but we made the most of every dollar for them. Even in the company's leanest years, when our services were put on hold, Clemons kept in touch.

We got to know his business very well, and I often shared some of my bigger ideas for how we could help them grow when they had the budget.

Then, suddenly, they had the budget.

"On the day we launched with Moderna," says Clemons, "it was easy for me to say, 'Dave, I don't know what we need. What I do know is I want to implement everything that we've talked about in the last four years as fast as possible.' Every good idea that we had was suddenly turned on."

Clemons didn't have to go searching for a marketing partner in the moment, because we already had a strong relationship.

"They understood our business," says Clemons. "They already knew what we wanted, so it's not like I was spending a year getting them to understand how I operate and what I need."

They didn't have a year. We were in the midst of a pandemic, and VitaLink had a chance to be part of the solution. Fortunately, they'd nurtured the right relationships before they needed them most, and that foundation allowed them to leap into action. They knew we were ready to do the same.

A 72-Hour Sprint Leads to Vastly Exceeding Recruitment Goals

After we got the call from VitaLink about the Moderna trial, we did a 72-hour sprint to start recruiting volunteers.

In those crucial hours, we built a dedicated landing page for the study on the patient-facing website. On the back end, we integrated ChatBot, CallRail, and Mailchimp into a master spreadsheet for the study, so that every call and submission were automatically added, and volunteers received immediate follow-up emails with additional study information.

We also launched an online advertising campaign, followed later by a TV advertising campaign.

We could do all this so rapidly because we had already developed the patient-facing site, the integrated digital infrastructure, and the automated design systems. We knew VitaLink well from years of partnerships. We had long ago prepared the way to launch large recruitment campaigns at speed.

With online advertising funneling traffic to the patient-facing website and underlying digital infrastructure, VitaLink was soon exceeding its weekly recruitment benchmarks. The original goal was to recruit 400 volunteers. By the end of the campaign we had added 5,000 patients to their database. After qualification, about 1,200 patients were chosen for the mRNA vaccine study, 400% of the original goal. Many more went on to participate in other studies.

With thousands of participants signing up, VitaLink activated all the systems it had developed for just such a need: They followed their SOPs and regulatory systems. They staffed up using the hiring and training systems they had put in place. They conducted dry runs and low-volume pilot periods. They activated the digital infrastructure we'd built for them, and they leaned on partners like us to rise quickly and ably to the challenge.

On December 18, 2020, the FDA granted the Moderna vaccine emergency use authorization, bringing hope to millions of Americans that the pandemic's end was in sight. VitaLink, a small by design company, had contributed mightily to this rapid result.

Operation Warp Speed Takes Notice

During the Moderna trial, VitaLink caught the attention of Operation

Warp Speed, a joint program of the Department of Health and Human Services, the CDC, the NIH, the Biomedical Advanced Research and Development Authority (BARDA), and the Department of Defense. The program sent their chief advisor, Moncef Slaoui, PhD, and their COO, General Gustave F. Perna to VitaLink to investigate.

"Afterwards, I got a call from Moderna," Clemons says. "They said that Warp Speed came down to observe us and two others like us that are independent, wholly-owned networks, to prove that they should have used only larger institutions."

However, they were so impressed by VitaLink's systems, and by how quickly they had scaled up to take on such an urgent trial, that they changed their mind.

"The project manager at Moderna said, 'Hey, we told them they were wrong, and you guys helped us prove that.'"

Operation Warp Speed went on to recommend further use of small by design clinical trial networks.

Following on that big success, in September of 2021 VitaLink was one of two multi-site clinical trial companies acquired by Velocity Clinical Research. These acquisitions have made Velocity the largest privately held clinical trial network in the world.

The acquisition was driven in part by VitaLink's impressive work on the Moderna trial, but Velocity was interested in more than those recruitment numbers. Like Operation Warp Speed, Velocity saw value in the systems that made those results possible. They're now integrating many of VitaLink's small by design practices into this much larger combined company, including VitaLink's patient recruitment system, and their extensive standard operating procedures.

"Having faced the same challenges as VitaLink when scaling up for Operation Warp Speed, we could certainly understand the difficulties and the magnitude of their success," says Dr. G. Paul Evans, President and CEO of Velocity. "When we started to engage with VitaLink, we could see immediately that they were a lean organization, the result of a deep understanding of what truly impacted the business. We are now taking a number of the systems that made VitaLink successful and scaling them to meet the needs of a larger business."

While the circumstances surrounding the Moderna trial were extraordinary, VitaLink's principles and practices gave them agility when the need arose. No matter how noisily opportunity knocks on your door, a foundation designed to scale empowers similar flexibility—and success.

But how do you sustain that success, not only during times of great opportunity but through the leaner times between? I have some thoughts on that in chapter 3.

Chapter 3:

SUSTAINABLE FINANCIAL ABUNDANCE

On Insomnia and Hating All Your Clients

"**I**'m working 80 to 90 hours a week. I'm making good money, but I'm exhausted all the time."

"I'm good at what I do. I love what I do. But I hate all my clients."

"I lie awake at night, worrying about where the money will come from next quarter."

To protect the open candor the above individuals bring to our conversations, I'm keeping their quotes anonymous, but this is a sampling of some of the concerns and complaints I've heard from small business owners who have come to me for advice.

No doubt about it: running a small business is hard work that comes with its share of stresses. Well-earned rewards require resilience and some strategic sacrifices. If "easy" is your goal, entrepreneurship simply isn't for you.

But when I hear that a small business owner isn't sleeping, or that all of their client relationships are thoroughly broken, I know something more serious is wrong. Because running a business on that kind of fuel simply isn't sustainable.

I hope it's clear to you by now that this book isn't a "get rich quick" guide for people who value their bank account balances above all else. While small by design principles do offer a path to financial rewards, it's one guided by payoffs that may not show up on your balance sheet: abundance of purpose and impact, of time and energy, of connection with family and friends… a life rich in all the ways that matter most to you.

Money does matter, and we're going to talk about it in this chapter. But let me say at the forefront—your pursuit of this abundance should never come at the cost of your health and happiness. And it doesn't have to, when you're small by design.

Don't Be Your Own Worst Boss

"When you start your own small business, chances are you've had a boss who was not a good steward of your time," says Michelle Waymire, founder of Young & Scrappy, a small by design financial services company. "We've all put up with a lot from bad bosses, but then all too often we step out and become our own worst bosses."

Waymire was determined to become her own best boss instead.

After earning her MBA in Finance, Waymire started out working for other companies in the financial services sector. The pay was good and the work was interesting, but something was missing.

"It was intellectually stimulating but emotionally unfulfilling," she says. "Selling financial products to rich people turned out not to be my favorite."

In her last job working for someone else, she respected and admired her colleagues. "It was a group of advisors, fiduciaries with a moral sense of the world, working hard to do right by clients," she says. But their business still wasn't aligned with her own vision: to serve young professionals, with a focus on the LGBTQ+ community.

She wanted her work to express and reflect the values she lived in the rest of her life. So she struck out on her own, starting Young & Scrappy to coach, advise, and assist her clients with everything from budgeting to business growth strategy.

Waymire counsels her business clients on much more than maximizing their net worth.

"You have to commit to making your business work for you, as a sustainable part of your life," she says, "rather than pouring everything into it, leading to burnout."

Burnout. That's what I heard when one small business owner told me, "I'm working 80 to 90 hours a week. I'm making good money, but I'm exhausted all the time." She's the same person who told me, "I'm good at what I do. I love what I do. But I hate all my clients."

These two complaints were completely connected, and the root cause was the same: she was being her own worst boss. Forcing herself to work unpaid overtime. Never pushing back when clients asked for too much. Failing to set and protect healthy limits and boundaries.

Perpetually overworked and exhausted, of course she started hating her clients. She received each new client request as another demand for time that wasn't available and energy she didn't have to give. But it didn't have to be that way.

"In good faith," says Waymire, "make sure you set yourself up to be the best boss you've ever had, instead of one more person you resent in your life."

That's the path to abundance your business can sustain.

Fretting About Finances is Normal

The financial stresses of running a small business are real. In urging you to focus on things beyond money, I'm not suggesting you ignore your company's finances altogether. Do that, and your entrepreneurial journey will be a short one.

You do need to pay attention to your finances, and there's a good chance you'll need some help understanding what you see. But it's beyond the scope of this book to explain how to read a balance sheet or P&L report, how to manage payroll and plan for taxes, or how to forecast your company's financial future.

My advice instead is simple: Find and develop a relationship with a good accountant, bookkeeper, financial planner, insurance broker, and corporate attorney. Do this immediately if you haven't done so already. And meet with them regularly to assess your company's present and future financial health.

Inevitably, sometimes what you learn from these experts will worry you. Worrying is completely normal. I hope you can take some comfort in knowing you're not alone. Some business leaders think they must always project confidence, but all of us worry about finances sometimes.

I wish I could tell you that the worry goes away eventually, but the truth is it never does. You just graduate to new kinds of worry. As a fellow entrepreneur once said to me, "New levels, new devils."

In the early days of your business, maybe you'll worry about affording a new laptop when your current computer is held together with duct tape and prayers. Later, maybe you'll worry about making payroll when your clients are paying their invoices late. If things go well, maybe someday you'll worry about whether you'll see any return on all the resources you invested in developing a new product.

It's all worry—and, I assure you, it's all normal.

As you may recall from chapter 1, in the early days of Ron Perry's launch of Perry Construction Management, he worried about making a mistake, getting audited, and then being shut down. In time, he came to realize that the government wasn't out to crush small businesses over minor mistakes.

Similarly, it's easy for your own financial concerns to spiral out of control—fearing bankruptcy and failure are just one accounting error away. But rest assured that most financial stresses are temporary and readily resolved. There's also no shame in reaching out for help.

Everyone running a small by design business has times when they have to draw on a line of credit to replace critical equipment, or get an advance on an invoice in order to make payroll. Every entrepreneur has taken a risk that didn't work out, and lost some money in the attempt.

None of this makes you a failure. None of it means your business is doomed to die.

There are, however, some things you can do to make such stresses less likely and more manageable when they do occur.

As Perry said, fear is a lack of knowledge. And knowledge is, ultimately, power.

"If you feel like there's never enough money, then know your numbers," says Waymire. "It may be easier to ignore numbers you don't know, but it's easier to panic too. Without knowing where your money goes, it's impossible to make change."

As a small by design business owner, you can have full transparency (with the help of your accountant and bookkeeper) into the financial health of your business. This powerful knowledge allows you to adapt and plan as you go.

Consider this: If you worked for someone else, the same financial risks would still exist, but you wouldn't know about them, so you couldn't do anything to address them. You'd just show up one day to find a pink slip and an empty cardboard box to pack your stuff into when the company had to lay you off.

As a small by design business owner, you will never show up to find that empty cardboard box. Because you can always know your numbers. Personally, I find that incredibly comforting.

During the fretful times, I also urge you to remember that you've already made it this far doing something you love, something other people agree that you're good at. That's an amazing accomplishment most people will never experience. So pause a moment and congratulate yourself, then roll up your sleeves and figure out how to move your business toward a less stressful, more sustainable financial abundance.

Run the Roots Deepest Where You Already Are

"I lie awake at night, worrying about where the money will come from next quarter."

The small business owner who said that to me was getting interesting projects and doing good work. His clients liked him, and he was making a profit. In the present, everything was fine. It was the future that wouldn't let him sleep.

While he had plenty of work, all of it was short-term and project-based. He had no idea what work would come next. What would he do when his current projects were completed? What if no new business materialized?

Always hustling for the next client, the next job, he was ever vigilant, chasing after every opportunity, and he struggled to turn it off when the workday was done.

The stress and sleep deprivation were wearing him down. It wasn't sustainable.

I pointed out to him that the easiest sales to make are to the clients you already have. They already know you, trust you, and like your work. (If they don't, that's a different problem.) And you already know them, so you know what they value and need.

New client sales take much more time and energy, usually with a lower rate of success. They're necessary to grow your business over time. But for sustainable abundance that doesn't wear you down, you should first run the roots deeper where you already are.

My advice to this business owner? Upsell, resell, and get them on retainer. Here's how you do that.

Offer More Value Than Requested

When your existing clients ask you to take on a project for them, consider how you could offer more value than they've requested.

Maybe your clients only have a narrow view of what your company can do and don't realize you're capable of more. Maybe they don't see the same opportunities you do to better serve their goals. Maybe they don't even realize more is possible.

Whatever the reason may be, assure them that you can deliver what they're requesting… then propose a higher fee to do even more, explaining the greater returns they can expect on their investment in your company's work.

If they accept the increase in scope, deliver well on all you've promised. This will set a new baseline for what they'll ask and expect of you in the future.

Surpass With Each Sequel

It's a hard dose of reality, but anything that impresses your clients the first time will become their baseline expectation for every project that follows. You can't just repeat the same successes, as complacency will first stagnate, then eventually kill, any client relationship.

Instead, with each new client project, ask yourself: "How can the sequel outperform our previous success?" Show them that there's still more to your agency than what they already know. Entice them to stick with you and discover what else you have to offer.

To illustrate: One of my agency's clients wanted to build a promotion around a national holiday related to their business. The first year, we did a photoshoot and developed some new digital content. The next year, we secured a relevant URL for them and got their site up to third place on search results for the event. The third year, we built them a branded video game.

Surpassing with each sequel keeps your existing client relationships strong and always growing.

Retainers Rule

Here's some more subtle math for sustainable financial abundance: A small, recurring retainer is more valuable than a large, one-time lump sum.

That's the advice I gave the small business owner who couldn't sleep. I told him to get his existing clients on any size retainer. $500 a month with a one-year commitment, I suggested, even as little as that.

This spoke directly to the cause of his insomnia. Many of his clients were, on average, paying him more than that per project, but without the assurances of reliable forthcoming revenue. Securing ongoing retainers would free him from worrying about where the money would come from next quarter. He could stop fretting about the future, plan forward, and let himself get some sleep.

But retainers give you more than baseline predictability. They also deepen and solidify relationships with your clients, almost always leading to work beyond what's initially scoped.

As I'll discuss at greater length in chapter 8, retainers are your ticket into higher-level, ongoing discussions with a client. Instead of waiting for them to come to you with requests, you're part of the conversations in which problems and opportunities arise. If your company can provide needed solutions—whether within the scope of your retainer or as an add-on project for an additional fee—your pitch to do so is easy. Their trust in you is already established.

Overages, additional projects outside the retainer, and, eventually, increases in your base retainer fee will grow your recurring revenue almost effortlessly—while letting you sleep better at night.

Happy Clients are a Compounding Investment

Investing deeply in your current clients is, in part, a strategy for growing your recurring revenue from those same clients. But the returns extend beyond that.

As you grow these relationships, delivering and receiving more value with each successive project, you're simultaneously investing in your clients' enthusiasm for your company. Happy existing clients will automatically start referring you to potential new ones, and the more happy clients you have, the more referrals you'll get.

Outside of upselling and reselling to your existing clients, warm recommendations are the second most efficient way to make a sale. Your clients will do much of the work for you, and their third-party endorsements will carry more weight than anything that you could say on your own behalf.

So invest in delivering reference-quality work to your clients, even if it reduces your profit margin in the short term. (I'll talk more in chapter 4 about how reference-quality work helps you tell your company's story effectively to attract new clients.) Ultimately, the impact of your best work will snowball into opportunities from client referrals, thereby multiplying your long-term gains.

It's not explosive growth, but it will compound over time. And as any financial advisor will tell you, compounding returns are the secret to long-term abundance.

Abundance is More Than Market Analysis

Financial stability takes more than good sales. It also relies on carefully curating the opportunities you pursue and accept. So how do you decide which clients and projects are worth your company's investment?

Sustainable abundance requires you to consider more than just the money you'll make from any given contract. Some clients won't be worth the sacrifices they require, and there are opportunity costs to working with clients who aren't a good fit for your business.

There's a famous decision-making matrix, first published by BCG in 1968 and taught to this day in business schools as a tool for strategic thinking. The BCG Growth Share Matrix[8] has two axes: market share and growth rate. The four quadrants of the matrix are "Stars," "Cash Cows," "Question Marks," and "Pets."

In the context of a small by design business, a "Star" is a client who is already profitable for you and who has the potential to grow with you even more.

A "Cash Cow" is one who is profitable and helps you pay the bills,

---

8   "What is the Growth Share Matrix?" Martin Reeves and Sandy Moose. Retrieved November 4, 2021 at https://www.bcg.com/about/overview/our-history/growth-share-matrix

but will likely never grow into much more.

A "Question Mark" is a client who isn't yet very profitable for you, but in whom you see real potential to grow into something more.

"Pets" aren't profitable now and probably never will be. If you keep them around, it's because you're attached to them in some way. Conventional business school wisdom says it's a strategic mistake, a failure of leadership, to keep these clients around... though I think that's not always true.

While the BCG matrix is useful, I think it's incomplete, especially for anyone staying small by design.

I have another matrix I consider in making these decisions—one that adds two additional dimensions to my decisions. Let's call it the Morale and Purpose Matrix.

Some clients are simply a pleasure for you and your team to work with. They're kind, appreciative, complimentary, and always pay you on time. While they might not give you the highest-dollar projects, they trust you, treat you with respect, love the work you do, and let you know it. These clients are good for your and your team's morale. They can be a playground for creative ideas, or at the very least a source of positive energy for your team.

Other clients align with your values and sense of purpose. Their mission is noble and their vision inspiring. The work you do for them feels important and meaningful. These clients are good for your soul.

A healthy heart and a satisfied soul serve your sustainability. You and your team won't mind the hard times as much when you love what you're doing and feel loved for it too. It's sometimes worth taking on low-growth, low-profit clients—the "Pets" in the BCG matrix who you're supposed to eliminate—if they make you feel good in those ways.

I have some of these clients at my agency. We don't make much of a profit off our work for them, and we probably never will. But my team and I feel so good about our work with them. That's its own kind of abundance.

I think that's true for any business owner, of any age, and anyone you hire. But with Millennials now the dominant demographic in the workforce and Generation Z on the rise, there's a trend toward prioritizing purpose over pay[9]. So if you want to attract the best talent to your company and inspire them to give their best, you have to consider more than market share.

That small business owner who hated all her clients? I told her she needed to find at least one client who told her all the time how much they love her and her work, even if they didn't pay her as much. Her market share and growth were doing just fine, but she needed a kind client to keep her morale high and refill her heart and soul.

Full bank accounts will only take you so far. For truly sustainable financial abundance, you need clients who give you purpose and make you happy too.

How else can you reap the rewards of your business without becoming your own worst boss? Here are some additional strategies that help you along the way to sustainable finances.

A Playbook for Financial Stability and Abundance

No One-And-Dones

Choose clients with the potential to develop into long-term relationships. Selling and negotiating is just too much work to go through for a single project with a client who you'll never work with again.

---

9   Understanding Generation Z in the Workplace," Tiffany Mawhinney and Kimberly Betts, Deloitte. Retrieved November 12, 2021 from https://www2. deloitte.com/us/en/pages/consumer-business/articles/understanding-generation-z-in-the-workplace.html

During the vetting and pitching process, ask clients about their long-term goals. Does your project feel like a one-time fix for them, or can you see yourself growing together?

Ask a lot of questions about their big picture strategy and vision. Reference larger projects you have done for other clients, and describe the value those clients have received. How does the potential client respond?

As I'll discuss at greater length in chapter 4, talk about your intended ideal outcome of this first project, and how it could lead to a "phase two." Do they seem open to that sequel? If so, you'll know you're both headed in a sustainable direction together.

Price Your Projects Right (and Establish Minimums)

Look up hourly rates of other service businesses in your industry, especially within your region. What's the range? What are the cost drivers?

Get a feel for what other companies are charging. What size are those companies? What do their websites look like? What is their perceived quality or eliteness? While you may not be able to charge the highest rate in town, their number is one you should work toward.

Meanwhile, what's the highest hourly rate you've ever charged for a project? Congratulations, that's your new baseline hourly rate!

Also learn to set and express a minimum project fee. This will save you so much time when qualifying potential clients, and it's the first step in upselling to a contract with greater impact and value.

Consider this: it's so much more efficient and profitable to win one $10,000 contract than twenty contracts at $500 each. The latter will eat up all your profit margin with sales, onboarding, and administration. Same goes for one $100,000 contract instead of ten contracts at $10,000.

The minimum fee you set will vary based on your industry and your own company's growth, but it should be high enough to disqualify all the work that will keep you busy without bringing you truly sustainable financial abundance.

Elastic is Fantastic

As I'll discuss more in chapter 6, your go-to team of contractors is key to your profitability. They're there when you need them—when there's billable work to be done. If you have a lull between big projects, or are in a phase where you're pitching new work and wrapping up other contracts, you're not on the hook to keep paying these contractors every two weeks. Your overhead can stay lighter without compromising quality or hurting your bottom line.

Share the Abundance

Profit sharing agreements get your whole team invested in your company's financial abundance. To keep good people around, incentivize them with a profit share or some other level of vested financial interest in the company.

Shortly after the COVID-19 pandemic started, entrepreneur Mark Cuban said on a podcast, "You will get more from your employees, and they will be more committed if you share equity immediately in a meaningful way, so that everybody rises up. No entrepreneur can do this alone. You need every single employee committed to helping you get through this, so recognize that. Reward them for it."[10]

---

10 "Mark Cuban says now is the time for CEOs to give stock options to everyone at the company," Graham Rapier, *Insider*, June 15, 2020. Retrieved November 12, 2021 from https://www.businessinsider.com/mark-cuban-says-ceos-should-give-all-employees-stock-options-2020-6

All of my employees get a profit share proportional to their role at the agency. They benefit from my company's sustainable financial abundance, and they're directly invested in nurturing it as we grow.

Sidebar: Best Practices for Abundance

As I mentioned at the beginning of this chapter, the intricacies of managing business finances are beyond the scope of this book. There are many other resources available to help you with all of that. But you can't go looking for information and support that you don't know you need. So I crowd-sourced a checklist of financial management advice from several entrepreneurs in my network.

I'm calling these financial best practices to your attention but won't attempt to explain them. If they're unfamiliar or confusing, you should seek out an expert who can help.

Most of these items come from two sources: Michelle Waymire, who I introduced earlier in this chapter. And Mitesh Patel, a financial analyst and business attorney who founded Blue Sky Law Group to help small businesses with financial management and compliance.

Financial Checklist

- As I mentioned earlier in this chapter, find a good financial planner, CPA, bookkeeper, insurance broker and corporate attorney. Each will have a direct impact on your financial health.
- Once you start hiring people, find a good payroll service.
- Track all of your income and expenses, and save all your receipts.
- If you use bookkeeping software, invest the time to learn how to use it, or invest the money in hiring someone else to manage it for you.

- Ask a qualified financial services professional to teach you how to read and understand your company's financial statements.
- Review these financial statements monthly, and make adjustments where needed.
- Set aside money to pay your taxes at the time when you earn the revenue.
- Get clear on the timing of quarterly taxes, and make a plan to pay those regularly to avoid penalties.
- Work toward saving up three to six months of operating expenses, and three to six months of personal expenses.
- Obtain a line of credit during good times. It's almost impossible to get one when you most desperately need it.
- Get an umbrella insurance policy, and, if relevant to your business, a cyber risk policy.
- Check your monthly subscriptions quarterly and determine which ones you are using and aren't (or forgot about). These costs add up fast!
- Pay yourself first. (That's what good bosses do.)
- Don't be afraid to ask for help.

On Better Sleep and Liking Your Clients

That small business owner who was always worrying about the next quarter's revenue? Soon after we talked, he signed his first retainer with one of his existing clients. It's small, but he knows now that he'll be paid every month. More retainers have followed, and likely all of them will grow.

He's sleeping better at night.

And the small business owner working 80 to 90 hours per week? She's now setting clearer boundaries with her clients, and providing more visibility into all the work she's doing for them. Now they understand when she pushes back on additional requests. She also now has some clients who tell her regularly how much they appreciate her work.

Recently she wrote to me: "I have been implementing your sage advice, and wow has it changed my perspective on everything. From how I'm setting up my team for next year, to how I interact with clients, to the way I see and value my own work—such a difference!"

Are they now living their best lives in lazy luxury while driving Lamborghinis? No, of course not. As I said earlier, entrepreneurship is never easy. They're ascending to new levels and discovering those new devils.

The work of running a small by design business is hard, and not all of it will be satisfying or firmly in your sweet spot. For many small business owners, financial management is neither. But learning to manage your money well is worth it. Do the work with diligence, and you'll be well on your way to abundance that's sustainable.

Sustainability has been the focus of the first section of this book: how to win the work, complete the work efficiently, and do it all in a way that supports your long-term health and happiness. In the next section, we'll examine how to amplify your impact while staying small by design. It all starts with a story.

SECTION TWO:

Impact by Design

Chapter 4:

START WITH THE STORY

From Big Three to Revolutionary

For his first few years after graduating with an MBA from the University of Chicago, Brad White had the kind of success many business school grads dream of. As a project leader at BCG[11], his future was bright at a Big Three management consulting firm. Working at the world's second largest such firm by revenue, he never lost sleep at night when it came to making payroll or convincing a potential client that his company could be counted on to complete the job. He was an avatar of BCG. Reliability was simply assumed.

---

11 I reference BCG's Growth Matrix in chapter 3.

"I started there because it was structured and low risk," he says. "It's a great place to learn, so I couldn't go wrong."

But White was restless at BCG. In those days the structure could be stifling, specialization was everything, and Adam Smith's capitalist division of labor ruled the day. White's curiosity and creativity wanted a less compartmentalized, more cross-functional environment.

He wanted to be part of a different kind of story. He wanted more than to be a part of it; he wanted to craft a new narrative himself.

So in 2004, he co-founded (r)evolution, a brand strategy, marketing, innovation, and growth consultancy that eventually grew to have a little over two dozen employees, an ensemble cast in which every character's voice and vision were vital. White and everyone he hired were involved in... everything, from putting new paper in the printer, to weighing in on brand growth strategy for major clients, and making decisions about the company's values and direction.

Together, they developed (r)evolution's story through the projects they pursued and the results they delivered for their clients. This was not an improvised, choose your own adventure. White knew the kind of stories he wanted to tell, and this knowledge guided every choice that he made along the way.

Sharing stirring tales of customer triumph with current and prospective clients, he established trust in his small by design startup's ability to grow major brands. And with that trust, (r)evolution grew to the point where the company was acquired by Prophet, a larger brand strategy firm.

Yet White's story was just beginning.

Stories Build Success and Stability

Stories are the great equalizers of entrepreneurial endeavors. They create meaning and connect you to clients without regard to the size of your workforce or annual gross revenue.

Each project becomes a building block of a more stable small. So you need to ask yourself from the beginning: what stories do you want to tell potential clients? What wins are you looking for? What other business do you want to attract?

Consider two small companies. Each takes on 10 projects in a year, at an average fee of $100,000, for a gross revenue of $1 million.

Company A says yes to whatever comes along. The projects don't cohere into a well-crafted larger story.

Company B goes after projects that fit in the overall narrative about their business. Nine of their ten projects end up supporting this story. (One doesn't, but helps pay the bills.)

In year two, company B will build more momentum than company A. They'll attract higher value projects from clients who connect to their story—clients better aligned with their values too.

Large companies can lean simply on numbers to sell their services. They can say, "We provide widget optimization services to 70 of the 100 largest widget producers on the S&P 500." Though they might win better business by telling good stories, numbers like this will keep the work flowing in.

But as a small by design company, you can't rely on client volume to sell your name. You need each project to serve a larger story. One of who you are and who you are becoming. A story of the crises you confront for your clients. Of the struggles that test your strength. A story of the value you deliver and the visions you make real.

When you tell that story well, in a way that connects to the needs and ambitions of your clients, they don't care if you're a company of one or one thousand. They care instead that you are the one who understands their unique needs and has proven you can help them succeed.

To be clear, I'm not talking about spin here. Your story has to be real—told through the work that you do and the value you deliver. But you do have to tell it well, with craft and intention.

In order to do that, you need each project to count. And to do that, you need to know where your story is going.

Start with the Story Arc

Since the dawn of TiVo in 1999 (then streaming services starting around 2007), we've been in what many people consider a Golden Age of TV. I bring this up not to encourage binge watching as a business strategy, but to point out a key shift in how the best television shows were crafted once viewers could reliably watch every single episode at their own convenience.

Prior to this time, most TV shows established a basic premise, setting, and cast of characters, then wrote and produced episodes crafted to stand alone. You didn't need to know what had happened last week. And this week's episode wasn't building toward anything happening next week. Each installment was essentially a reboot: same characters, same idea, but pay no attention to whatever came before, and expect no continuity with what we'll do next week.

Many businesses work the same way. They have a basic brand and a service they provide. They have a team of leaders and employees, and an office building where you'll often find them doing their work.

But the projects they take on stand alone. The company does the work, collects the fees, then moves on to the next job with no sense of connection or progression.

Consider instead a show like "Breaking Bad," in which the hapless chemistry teacher Walter White, as we meet him in the show's first episode, bears little resemblance to the ruthless drug lord Heisenberg he becomes. His transformation over the show's five-year run was central to its appeal.

Crucially, this worked because the show's creators knew the broad strokes of the character's transformation long before the first day of filming. Every episode was a continuation of what had come before and supported where the show was going next. Writers knew the full story arc from the beginning, and that's an important part of what made "Breaking Bad" great.

Something similar happened with the "Infinity Saga" in the Marvel Cinematic Universe. Twenty-three films in three phases over eleven years all served the story arc that culminated in "Avengers: Endgame," one of the most ambitious cinematic achievements in film history. Here, too, the creators knew the story arc they wanted to tell from the beginning. They never would have achieved the impact of "Endgame" had they just made a bunch of superhero movies (even with linked characters) without a larger narrative plan.

Great companies of all sizes use similar story arcs, and for small by design companies they are essential for success and stability.

Here's how you can tell a story well through the work that you do.

A Playbook for Writing the Story of Your Success

Pursue the Three-Act Plays

Like most good theater, a good story about your small by design business will have three acts, sometimes referred to as the Beginning, Escalation, and Conclusion. As you're considering which projects and clients to pursue, ask yourself whether they offer all three.

(r)evolution's earliest story came from Dixie®.

"We won that client based on the strength of relationships," says White. (See chapter 9 for much more on the importance of relationships.) "We had someone who liked the idea that we were starting up something new. He told us, 'I believe in you guys. I have a project for you, and I'd love to help you get started.'" This was the Beginning.

The project was to reposition the Dixie® cups brand. White knew that success with this client would be transformative for (r)evolution, establishing them as an agency that could be trusted with a major international brand and budget. So he and his partner pulled out all the stops. This was the Escalation.

"We hired additional writers and creatives. We worked late nights and weekends. We took the client out to nice dinners," says White. "Whatever it took to make sure it was a success. We made little or no profit, but profit wasn't the purpose of this project."

This investment yielded good results for White and his team, leading to a triumphant Conclusion.

"We had an aha moment during the project: a critical new insight about their customers," says White, "then we built their new positioning around that key insight. We handed it off to their team to put into practice. They did a great job, and, after the repositioning, their brand outperformed their original 12-month plan for years afterward."

It was a breakthrough success story for (r)evolution, and one they told repeatedly as they continued to grow. Why should a big brand trust this startup brand strategy agency? Because they had more than a logo and a quote from a household name. They had a good story to tell about a big challenge, an escalating effort, and a victorious conclusion.

Design for a Dramatic Climax

How do you know which projects have the potential to become a good three-act story? Look for the challenges that will give your story a dramatic climax: an intense and exciting turning point that leads to a satisfying conclusion.

"You need to go after reference-quality work," says White, "which has three essential elements: Insight, practice, and results."

Let's look at each element a little closer.

Insight. "Reference-quality work" starts with a big idea, a break-through moment, an experience of "aha"—just like the one White had with Dixie®. Your company gains an insight or offers a fresh perspective that changes how your client thinks about the problem, and therefore reveals a better solution.

Practice. A great idea that goes nowhere is a disappointment for all. No matter how staggeringly brilliant your insight is, will your client implement it? Can they? Or will they insist on less ambitious, more conventional approaches? Look for clients who have not only the vision to see the promise of your best ideas, but the operational systems to support them and the resources that will make them real.

Results. When the job is done, will you be able to show that your work made a difference? This may mean tracking and demonstrating quantifiable results, but that's not the only way. Results can be stories too: testimonials about how someone's job was transformed for the better, or gratitudes from customers who noticed and appreciated the new experience.

Insight, practice, and results. When you have all three, then you have the raw materials you need to craft a compelling climax and con-clusion to your story. Tell it well, and you'll inspire future clients, who will want to be a part of your next story of a dramatic turning point and happy ending.

Cast Your Characters Well

Directors are critical to the success of any film, but aside from the occasional handheld film school project, they don't create movies alone. One of the most important decisions directors make is determining which actors to cast in the film's key roles. This is essential, because the best actors don't just do what they're told—they embrace the director's vision and the script's story and characters, and they work hard to bring all of it alive.

Similarly, when you're choosing partners, employees, and contractors for your small by design business, make sure you cast people who will help you bring your story to life.

"When we hired people at (r)evolution," White says, "we'd tell them, 'You'll be one of, say, 13 voices shaping our processes, strategies and culture.' We looked for people who had a passion for that, people who found joy in the entrepreneurial spirit."

Like a good director, (r)evolution hired people who were inspired by their story, and were eager to tell it well. People who had ideas of their own and wanted to contribute. Like White in his early days at BCG, they were individuals, he says, who didn't want to "stay in their swim lane."

Not everyone wants that boundless open-water freedom. Some like the security and stability of a well-defined role at an established company that already has all its systems and culture in place. They prefer to read the stories that others have already written. There's nothing wrong with that, but such people probably won't thrive at a small by design company.

Simply put: you need the storytellers.

Plan a Story Your Clients Will Tell

Your clients are your very best storytellers.

Maybe you read that last line and said, "Well, other than me! I'm clearly the best person to tell my story, then my clients can help."

But I really do mean that you are often not the best person to tell your company's story. As the person who stands to gain most from a flattering version of yourself, you will often be seen as an unreliable narrator.

That's why third-party endorsements are so powerful in marketing, and it's why your clients are more trusted narrators. They know you well, yet they are not you, so they can tell your story with greater authority.

Now, to be clear, when your clients tell these stories, they will be tales of their own triumph. This is as it should be, even if you were the storyteller who scripted their success. That's your job: to give them opportunities to be stars, so they'll keep coming back for more. Prospective new clients will want you to write such starring roles for them. So don't expect your clients to tell a story in which you're the hero.

That's not to say you don't have a role in crafting what they tell; exactly the opposite. If you've ever had a client refer you to another prospect, you've probably had moments of slightly cringing inside with a smile plastered on your face, while your client, with the best of intentions, misrepresented what your company does and the value you have to offer.

You should absolutely help your clients tell the story accurately and well. Do so by developing a narrative arc that will be clear to them. Call it to their attention regularly throughout your engagement. Don't just do the work. Show them how the work fits into the larger tale.

For example...

- Are you connecting your client's website to some third-party web services? No, you're building an integrated digital experience platform for their customers, and here are all the enhancements and efficiencies that came from that...
- Are you checking off items on a punch list for a new factory's construction? No, you're holding the shared vision of all

the stakeholders in a construction project, and helping them bring it to life.

- Hanging new signs in a residential development? No, you're helping a community transform to a new understanding of its purpose.

As you work on each project, let the clients know how you are taking everything into consideration—how it all connects and what the big picture implications are. Some of this may seem obvious to you, but it may not be obvious to them.

Always keep in mind that your project is larger than the sum of individual tasks. You should know what that greater sum is, and communicate it to your clients throughout the whole project. Why? Because that's how they will tell the story of working with you—the story you want them to tell. And there is nothing more powerful than having your client tell it well.

Plan Your Plot Points

What kinds of client projects make up the chapters of your company's story? Yes, it's important to diversify, but what's the thread that connects them? As you plan for the future, what are the unifying threads you want?

Some of the connective tissue may be an industry (e.g. manufacturing, medical research, or restaurants), but think beyond that too. Do you want to tell the story that you work with Fortune 500 companies but also enjoy working with locals? Or is it that you like focusing on projects in higher education, and also do a pro-bono project for a small educational establishment every year? Do you invest deeply in your community by serving only companies based in your city? Or do you leverage information technology to serve clients all over the world?

What kind of business do you want to be known as? Make sure you pursue the clients and projects that will help you tell that tale.

Choose Storylines That You Want Others to Make Real

The stories you tell will influence not only your company's path, but also the work of your people and their growth.

One of my agency's stories is that we are champions of accessible website design that makes the Internet better for everyone. We insist on using this approach on every project we do, even when the client isn't concerned about it.

Because I mapped out that arc for our business, told it again and again, and live it in the work we do, one of my developers has deeply studied accessible design and become an expert in it. He now challenges me to push our projects even further toward universal accessibility. I started the story, but he's making it even more real.

As a result, my whole team now not only thinks about and tells this story, but helps it expand through their own dedication. By taking on our company narrative as their own, their individual expertise increases, and consequently we deliver more value to our clients.

Write Down the Conclusion Before You Begin

I've already mentioned how results and satisfying conclusions are important, which is why I encourage you to write down your fairytale happy ending before you even agree to project. Put it on paper: "By doing this project we were able to achieve X for the client by doing Y in Z time." Visualize the project's completion, and every task it takes to get there. Will this give you the raw materials for a good story? If the answer is yes, work toward that powerful conclusion every step of the way.

If you aren't able to see or articulate this vision, you should strongly consider why you are agreeing to the work in the first place.

As I discussed in chapter 3, it's truly okay if the answer is, "This one pays the bills." But if that's the case, it needs to pay WELL.

The key here is not just to know when to say no. (I'll talk more about that in chapter 7.) Writing down the conclusion gives you the foresight you need to plan for that happy ending and a story that you and your client will both be delighted to tell.

The Story of the Paratrooper

Brad White's own professional story is told across not just one company but several, like a popular protagonist hero in a series of books. He's not merely a part of BCG, or (r)evolution, or Prophet. He's not just Brighthouse: a company that BCG bought then recruited White back to lead as an independently operating creative agency. He's not defined by his latest leadership role at Decisely, a tech startup disrupting HR management and employee benefits for small companies.

White is more than any of those companies, large or small. He's the leader who can drop into an organization that's new or not yet fully defined. Then he can lead it to growth and success.

His story is a parable about a paratrooper.

"Since 2005, I've parachuted into four early stage small companies or small divisions within companies, and helped them grow," White says. "You have only what you brought with you, not a lot of support or infrastructure. You and your team are on your own for a bit, and you have to figure it out with limited resources."

White lands in organizations with a mission but no clear road map of how to get there. Paratroopers don't need roads, and that's exactly how he likes it.

"This is what attracts me to small organizations," he says. "You can create your own vision, your own way forward. Then you build it."

In other words, he enjoys leading companies whose narrative arcs have not yet been drawn, then defining them with strategically chosen stories told well, through the triumphs of their clients. That's part of why the businesses he has founded and led have been so successful.

Those successes are also chapters in White's own ongoing professional journey. Investors, clients, co-founders, employers, and essential team members know that he is the visionary, the serial storyteller who can guide organizations forward through unmapped lands. And each story in his saga opens up new opportunities for him: another plane to jump out of with a parachute strapped to his back, and a new quest for client growth and glory.

The story of your own small by design business is inextricably also a story about you. Maybe it's a story that continues and develops beyond your first business. Make it a good story. It's the story of you.

Then take what you learn about those unmapped lands, and lead the way forward for those who want to follow. I'll talk more about that in chapter 5.

THOUGHT LEADERS COME IN ALL SIZES

Thoughts About Pie

"It all started over a piece of pie," says Margot Eddy, co-founder and COO of Imagine Media, a social media consulting firm.

In the early days of their company, Eddy and Shantel Kriss (co-founder and CEO) worked out of a nearby Panera Bread, surrounded by other small business owners also furiously working on their own laptops. Eddy and Kriss made a point of getting to know this ad hoc community of fellow entrepreneurs, listening to their struggles and answering their questions about the emerging opportunities for social media marketing to help small businesses grow.

Within this microcosm of carb- and coffee-fueled entrepreneurs, they developed a reputation as the people who understood how social media was evolving, people with a clear vision of how these platforms could drive small business growth. Their community turned to them for insights and advice.

Eddy and Kriss became social media thought leaders.

"We talked with people to hear what they needed to learn," says Eddy. "We were taking pictures of them and posting about them before social media was big."

One of these local businesses was a pie shop, run as a one-woman operation. "The product was amazing," says Eddy, "but there was nothing online about them. Are they open? What hours? We realized the owner was always in the kitchen, and the last thing on her mind was being on social media or marketing her services."

So Eddy and Kriss approached the pie shop owner, offering to handle social media for her. She accepted, and delectable social media photos of pie were soon bringing new business through the door. Imagine Media was officially in business, and their success with one client soon led to more, with about ten more small businesses signing on within the next few months.

Small Company, Big Ideas

Thought leadership is not just about proving you know how to use social media (or passing whatever quiz is most relevant to your field). It's not a resume or a credential that affirms you know what you're supposed to know. No matter the size of your company, thought leadership is the means by which you show that you have big ideas that are valuable to the people you're trying to reach.

Thought leadership can include sharing ideas that go contrary to conventional wisdom, but it doesn't have to. You can also…

- Think more deeply than others in your field, down to first principles and foundational ideas
- Craft a more comprehensive, global view that connects your specialty to larger ideas or a broader context
- Develop early expertise in a new or emerging topic in your industry that few people yet understand
- Ask compelling questions no one else is asking, including questions to which you don't necessarily have the answers

And thought leadership is something you share, as Eddy and Kriss did with the small business community they developed at Panera Bread. Protecting your proprietary process from any outside eyes may be a smart business decision in some cases, but it's not thought leadership.

"It's about how you contribute to society and your community at large," says Eddy, "adding value around that. I'm always talking about social media, [which] helps build that community around me."

Thought leadership inspires and lives in conversations. It shares knowledge, helping everyone do better, not just you. It's not: "Look at how good I am." Instead, it's: "Let's talk about how we can all do better."

Quality Ideas Matter More Than Company Size

Thought leadership doesn't necessarily serve every business or even every business owner's goals. If you're content to grow by word of mouth and organic reputation, you might not need a thought leadership strategy. Do good work, and trust it will inspire customer retention and word-of-mouth sales. That's a fine way to operate.

But if your growth goals are more ambitious, a thought leadership strategy can even out the playing field that big brands otherwise dominate with overwhelming numbers. There's that old saying (a cliche by now): "No one ever got fired for buying IBM." While IBM does quite a lot to enhance and amplify its reputation as a thought leader in technology, particularly technology as a business service, potential buyers come to a conversation with them already trusting they're leaders in this space—with tens of thousands of scientists and engineers backing up that reputation.

Your small by design business has no such luxury. You say you know what you're talking about, but do you? You have no army of experts standing behind you.

Thought leadership gives a decisive answer to the question of your expertise. And it goes beyond competence. Through it, you show you're not merely capable in your profession. You're someone leading the conversations, driving everyone to do better.

When you establish yourself as a thought leader, the size of your company becomes irrelevant. Potential clients focus instead on the quality of your ideas.

The Power of Your Best Thinking

Engaging in thought leadership will also help you during the sales and delivery cycle. Consider that a thought leadership strategy can:

- Open a conversation, whether organically in person, or after someone reads an opinion piece you wrote or listens to a talk you've given. It can generate warm, inbound leads from people who are already impressed by your thinking.
- Vet potential clients. Write and speak clearly and boldly about your most important values and beliefs. If prospective clients aren't well aligned with those values, you'll both discover that early, saving you both wasted time and unnecessary stress.

- Nurture a sales lead when the prospect is interested but not yet sure you can deliver. If you send them an article you wrote on a topic relevant to their needs, you'll further the conversation.
- Guide a prospective customer or client from what they say they want to what you know they actually need, helping them achieve their goals and become satisfied customers.
- Close a deal. When included with a final proposal or contract, your thought leadership pieces will help demonstrate why you are the one right person to lead this project.
- Support a successful client relationship and project by educating the client about what leads to that success.
- Keep the conversation going with a past client or customer who may need you again, or may refer you to someone in their network.

Establishing yourself as a thought leader also puts you in a new category for the prices you can charge. It builds your clout, which justifies your higher prices.

You prove you're not simply providing a commodity service. You're someone who sets and raises the standard for quality and value. You're not a service provider selling deliverables. You're a consultant who will steer clients toward the best choices in your field, and then deliver what you've shown them they need.

Clients come to a vendor for a product or service they've already defined, and they pay them to provide that service. But as a thought leader, you're not a vendor. You're a consultant who helps them understand what they actually need... and then delivers. You drive the conversation at least as much as the client, maybe more. And that means you can better steer everyone toward a successful outcome.

Thought leadership will also put your clients at ease. When my clients are anxious about some aspect of a project, I have a magic phrase: "Check out this article I wrote in Forbes about this." They're overcome with relief. They know they picked the right team, the right person.

Where Will You Lead?

You don't have to have a column in Forbes, Barron's, or the Harvard Business Review to be a thought leader. You don't have to give a TED talk or a keynote at Davos. (Though all of those certainly can help.)

We live in an era in which it is easier than ever to share your ideas and connect with the right audiences. The endorsement of respected gatekeepers of ideas certainly helps, if you can get it, but great ideas can serve your success even if you're publishing on Medium or presenting your own webinar.

It's the ideas that count the most.

Find topics you love and nerd out about, then go really deep on them.

And be mindful of your goals. Who are you trying to reach? What topics do they care about? What questions are they asking? What challenges are they trying to solve? Choose your topics and express your views with intention toward, as I discussed in chapter 4, the story you want to tell about your company.

Here's how to make the most of a thought leadership strategy.

A Playbook for Establishing and Amplifying Thought Leadership

Play to Your Passions

While thought leadership may be a business strategy, it should come from a place of passion.

"There's nothing worse than thought leadership that you feel like you have to be doing," says Eddy. "Start with what you'll be excited to talk about. Don't chase after a topic that has no spark for you. If you struggle trying to decide what the subject is, ask what gives you energy, what gets you excited?"

For Imagine Media, that passion was the emerging opportunity for social media to help small businesses reach a wide audience without a big marketing budget. Eddy and Kriss were authentically interested in the struggles of small businesses and genuinely excited about the new possibilities offered by social media marketing.

"Passion led the way," says Eddy.

Consider the Conversations You're Already Having

What are the questions that clients or colleagues keep asking you? What are the questions where you just go into your memory bank, and push play on your pre-recorded talk track?

Maybe it's time to write down that talk track and publish it, or deliver it in a speech.

I think this is particularly important when questions arise that might be somewhat contentious. It allows you to say, "I totally understand the pain point you are feeling, and I actually wrote an article about it because it comes up so often that I have been thinking a lot about it."

It saves you time, and it shows that you are reflective and seasoned: a thought leader.

Conversations are also how you learn what questions or struggles are most on the minds of the people you want to reach.

After Imagine Media was up and running, Eddy and Kriss worked for several years in a co-work space. There, they continued the same practices that had served them so well at Panera: they discussed social media developments and strategy with their colleagues in the space.

"We became the go-to people for social media advice," says Eddy, "and that led to a lot of conversations, grabbing coffee with people who wanted to ask us questions about social media. Most of our sales leads during that time came from conversations over coffee or happy hour."

At the intersection of their own passions and these discussions with colleagues, Imagine Media found their sweet spot for thought leadership.

"What do people come to you for advice about?" Eddy asks. "It doesn't have to be an orchestrated strategy. What do you find yourself talking about most?"

Be Humble (It's OK to Say You Don't Know)

You don't have to be a PhD or write a dissertation on a topic. You can say, "I don't really know the answer, but here is what I've learned."

Why is this important? It humanizes you.

You work in the professional services field, and part of your job will be teaching, explaining and listening. So it's good to say that you don't have all the answers, but then show that you have been paying a lot of attention to what has been going on. Show that you have an opinion, but that you are open to ideas.

And it's okay to put out content that says, "I don't know, but I am listening."

Tie It Back to Your Company's Culture

Putting out content with your name behind it also puts your personality, beliefs, and values out into the world. This is a great opportunity for someone to read or view your piece, then say, "I like this person's approach and the culture they are building." Always ask yourself if your thought leadership content aligns with your company culture.

Tailor It to Your Audiences

Thought leadership isn't just about whatever ideas happen to be of interest to you. Your thinking needs to have value to the people you're trying to reach. Effective thought leadership makes that value clear and easy to see.

You may even find yourself expressing the same ideas in multiple ways to connect them to different target audiences.

For example, I've spoken and written about accessible website design for audiences including business owners, agency owners, developers, and designers. My core ideas on the topic remain the same—accessible website design makes the web better for everyone—but the shape and content of my messages are tailored to what's most valuable to each audience.

For the past nine years, Imagine Media has sent out a weekly newsletter about social media. It shares their take on the latest news around the topic, highlighting what's most important in what can be an overwhelming sea of information.

The standard version of their newsletter goes out to a large list, the community they've built up since those early days working out of Panera. But two days prior, they send a different version exclusively to their clients. This newsletter has additional content and insights tailored to their clients' interests, with updates on how the Imagine Media team is adjusting social strategies to the latest developments.

So stay true to your own passions, the integrity of your best ideas. Then consider how you can best draw a connection between your thinking and the perspectives of your target audiences. Craft all your thought leadership content and conversations to make those connections.

Thought Leadership Can Be a Little Contrarian

Do you hold a unique opinion on a topic? Talk about it!

Now, I'm not talking about being contrarian for the sake of seeming singularly revolutionary and rare. This isn't your opportunity to playact the part of a rebel daring to step dangerously outside the walls of conventional wisdom. Rather, it's about expressing your genuine beliefs, without compromise or apology.

This is important because it encourages discourse within your community of peers. As I've previously mentioned, it's also a great vetting tool for potential clients. If they are aligned with your views, that's a great step in a good direction together. If it opens up disagreement, maybe this isn't the right fit.

Remember that this content you are producing is a lens into what it's like to work with you and your company—use it as a magnet to attract the right clients for you.

Go Deep Into Micro-Topics and Become a Micro-Expert

As you grow in your career, you'll start to dive deeply into specific topics with clients and become a mini-expert. This specific expertise can win you initial projects that can lead to larger work. (I'll say much more about starting small then going deep in chapter 8.)

As you nerd out on a topic, take note of what you learn. Start to write about it, post about it on social media, and become known as a thought leader not in your broad, general industry, but on a micro-topic within it. Leading the field can come later, built on the foundation of the smaller bricks of thinking you've mastered along the way.

Micro-topic thought leadership is also a great opportunity to get a foot in the door for a much larger project. As I'll describe later in this chapter, thought leadership in accessible web design and ADA compliance won my agency a major website contract.

Imagine Media made no attempt to compete as thought leaders in branding, marketing, and advertising. Their competitors are mostly large marketing agencies where social media is a tiny subset of all that they do. In contrast, social media is all that Imagine Media does, and their expertise within it runs deep.

Which social media platforms should a small retail clothing business be on? How can a regional restaurant chain make the best use of sharing video? The thought leaders at Imagine Media consider questions like these every day. And whenever a new platform takes off in popularity, they think about that too, then share their insights with their community, network, and clients.

"We get the businesses that want someone who specializes in social," says Eddy, "and they know exactly what we do well."

Eddy and Kriss don't have to position themselves as experts in marketing. They can compete with the big names on equal footing in the specialty they've staked out for themselves.

Think About Where Your Content Should Go

Just as you do with every project you take on and every hire you make, think about where each piece of thought leadership is best placed. And try to get the most mileage possible from each.

It's not just what you publish or present. What will you do with it after?

What do you want to accomplish through your thought leadership strategy? Attract talent? Get speaking gigs? Land a specific client? Is it a networking tool—more about who you connect with, through interviews and conversations, while creating it?

While you're pondering, here are some of the ways you might share your thought leadership content:

- Share it with your social network.
- Email it to your business network.
- Post about it on your website.
- Invite people to your speeches.
- Invite people to be on your panels.
- Invite people to contribute their ideas to your webinar, column, book, etc. (Open conversations and relationships even in the crafting of thought leadership content, as I did while writing this book.)
- Include it in your sales proposals.
- Include it at key points in your delivery process. (For example, if you write a piece about stakeholder engagement, utilize it at the kickoff of the discovery process to explain why you want to include the voices of other key stakeholders.)

As a social media consultancy, Imagine Media naturally posts thought leadership content to all the major social media platforms, though they speak to different audiences on different channels. "Instagram is mostly college kids looking for jobs," says Eddy, "so we try to inform them and help them with their next position. It's also good for our hiring and recruiting."

They also publish regularly on their blog, offering their best advice on common social media concerns. Some recent topics include, "Your Guide to Instagram Reels," "How to Grow Your YouTube Audience," and "Facebook Bulletin: A New Way to Engage."

"Blog posts and case studies are mostly for prospective clients," says Eddy. "They end with a takeaway readers can use, or they can call us for help."

For marketing professionals, Imagine Media offers a free webinar series, "Social Sessions." It's not a big lead generator, as most of their clients come from referrals. But because the series positions them as thought leaders in social media, it helps them close the deals once referrals are made.

"All of those combined have helped us get on the speaker's circuit," says Eddy. "When AmericasMart[12] is in Atlanta, they have us speak on social media to all the business owners, spreading our reputation nationwide."

[Sidebar]

Case Studies

Some people consider case studies a form of thought leadership, but I don't view them that way. (Hey, contrarian point!)

Case studies are an extension of having a logo on your site. They prove you know what you're doing, and that you can get the job done. Include a client testimonial in there and some impressive data. It's all important, but it's not furthering the conversation in your industry.

These in-depth accounts of client projects you've completed can provide the raw material for thought leadership. They are examples. Further reading. But your thought leadership must go deeper, connecting the specific example to some larger question or thesis.

So case studies are definitely valuable, but they're not thought leadership. Disagree? Let's have a conversation about that!

---

12 Located in downtown Atlanta, AmericasMart is one of the world's largest permanent wholesale marketplaces, with 7.2 million square feet across three buildings. The venue hosts a year-round series of markets that draw wholesalers and retail buyers from across the United States.

How Micro-Topic Expertise Opened the Door to a Big Client

A few years ago, I had an early conversation with a potential client. They were concerned that their website might not be in compliance with the legal requirements of the Americans with Disabilities Act (ADA).

It was a micro-topic I already knew quite a lot about, but I hadn't yet put myself out there as a thought leader in website accessibility.

I gave the client a quote for what it would take to bring the company website into compliance. Given the legal stakes, the quote was very reasonable but still a substantial investment for what probably felt to him more like insurance than a value-add. (I disagree with that calculus, but that's another story for another time.)

He found some plug-in he could use instead, for much less money. Only it wasn't actually any good. It gave them a false sense of confidence but missed much of what was wrong about their site.

Over the next year or two, I wrote several articles on website accessibility, including a high-level column on the topic in Forbes, making my case that accessible web design actually makes websites better for everyone and helps businesses grow. I also wrote a series of articles on best practices for accessible web design in Torque, a publication for web developers put out by WPEngine.

A couple years after the initial conversation with that potential client, they hired a new digital director. He got in touch with me and said, "Hey, I think this plug-in might not protect us from litigation."

He was right, and I told him so. I explained to him some of the deeper problems I'd seen with their website's accessibility, and told him that the plug-in couldn't address them. They needed a more fundamental rebuild.

I followed up afterward by sending him all the articles I'd written, which he then circulated within the company. One of the people who read them was the CFO. They began to see accessibility not as just a marketing issue. It was more important than that for their company. They were so convinced of this that they agreed the cost of their website compliance would not come out of the marketing budget. This was a capital expenditure, a long-term investment in their company's stability and growth.

My contact came back to me. "Give us a full quote, and tell us everything we need to do to do it right."

He was turning to me not as a commodity vendor, who could be underpriced by a cheaper option. He saw me as the person he could trust to tell him what the company needed. So I sent him a new quote, five times the original budget I'd proposed a couple years ago. A budget that would allow us to build a website that would be fully accessible and, as I'd already convinced him, better for everyone... better for business too.

They were now convinced that I was a thought leader in accessible web design. My articles had done that work for me. They trusted my advice and knew I was worth the price.

They accepted my offer.

Acquisition by Acadia

Image Media was recently acquired by Acadia, a trusted growth platform that applies technology, digital expertise, and co-investment to help brands out-flank their competition. Around the same time, Acadia also acquired two other companies: a web design agency specializing in Shopify implementations, and an SEO consultancy.

All three organizations were attractive acquisitions because they were thought leaders in their micro-topics. Acadia didn't need more people on the payroll. They needed deep expertise in very specific areas critical to their overall business strategy. So they went out and found the companies that had already established themselves as thought leaders in those fields.

The newly augmented company is now a little larger, but still much smaller than the big name agencies. Acadia sees that as a benefit.

"We are small by design, and our combined forces are more powerful than the average 'big' agency," says Eddy. "Our expertise allows us to manage the marketing strategy for mid-market disruptors who would be forgotten at a big agency, but would otherwise have to balance multiple agency partnerships to get the tailored strategies they need."

Because of their thought leadership, Imagine Media has become a part of something larger, but as you can see, they're still very much small by design, serving their clients well with the power of their best thinking.

What questions are most compelling to you? What micro-topics do you know better than anyone else? How do you want to drive your entire industry to do better? Where will you lead your field?

Share your questions and your best ideas. Your success will follow where your best thinking leads.

It's all going to lead to a lot of growth and change for your company, so you'll need to be ready to stretch and adapt as new opportunities and challenges come your way. I'll talk about how to do that in chapter 6.

Chapter 6:

ELASTICITY IS ESSENTIAL

After the Bubble Burst

I n the nineties, Peter Baron spent eight years building up his company, SocketPR, a traditionally structured public relations and marketing firm that served rapid growth tech companies. Then, in 2000, the dotcom bubble burst.

In the aftermath, Baron and his partner had to lay off a lot of people and were struggling to cover their fixed overhead. Luckily, an international PR and communications firm with over 2,000 employees bought them out, and for the next four years Baron worked as a general manager of the firm's Atlanta office.

The acquisition brought stability and financial rewards in a dire economic environment, but Baron wasn't happy with how it changed their client relationships.

"The company only wanted big accounts and then to grow them," says Baron. "Any loyalty to the cause of the client was feigned. They had enthusiasm for making money; that's all."

But with a massive payroll and overhead to cover each month, the company needed those big accounts to keep the big checks coming. There was simply no flexibility in the system to adjust their costs and capacity to revenue fluctuations. They had no elasticity, so making money ruled each day.

When Baron left the company in 2004 to start a second new agency of his own, he vowed, "I'm never going to do it like this again."

Elasticity is Essential

Elasticity is essential when you're small by design.

Elasticity is how a small company stretches to take on big or urgent projects. It's also how you shrink your costs when business is slow.

Elasticity is how you level up to take on new challenges above and beyond your own experience. It's also how you engage the expertise of seasoned professionals whose salaries you could never afford.

Small by design can remain stable and strong through fluctuations in opportunities and revenue, as long as you can adapt your costs and capacity as you go.

When Baron founded Carabiner Communications, he didn't lease any office space, and he didn't hire employees. He'd learned those things can keep you from being nimble. Instead, he reached out to highly skilled contractors he'd met throughout his career. He didn't offer them full-time employment, as most would (understandably) command veteran salaries his young company could not afford. He asked them instead to join his team of contractors —"Carabiners," he likes to call them—people he would turn to as client needs and budgets allowed.

At the time, he thought it was a temporary solution until Carabiner became better established. He imagined he would eventually find office space and start hiring. But that temporary solution worked out better than he had ever imagined—in part because of the elasticity it afforded.

"People preferred being superstars without full-time commitments," he says. "Clients liked it better too." Seventeen years later, they're still operating this way.

Tap Into a Global Talent Pool

Baron challenges the conventional wisdom that companies need lots of employees to serve their clients well. He believes that Carabiner's reliance on extraordinary contractors allows him to deliver superior service.

"It's about working with brilliant people," he says, "rather than a big brand where the interns are doing all the work for a couple of gray hairs at the top. Large agencies are unable to compete with us, because they can't build a staff of superstars. It's too expensive for them. They hire stars-in-development."

As I write this, it's a golden age for hiring skilled contractors. Never has the talent pool been so wide and deep, so global, and yet so effortless to engage. But like all the strengths of staying small by design, effective elasticity doesn't happen just because you outsource to contractors.

Farm everything out to the lowest bidder, and you'll end up delivering lowest bidder results to your soon dwindling list of clients. Even contractors with exceptional skills need the right systems in place to deliver their superior results. And while you won't necessarily have to manage the day-to-days of office politics, contractors are still people who will serve your success best when treated well and given good reason to care.

Here's how both Baron and I build, nurture, and deploy an elastic team ready to leap into action whenever our clients need their elite skills.

The Contractors Playbook

Evaluate What Must Be Handled In-House

Not everything can be outsourced, or at least not everything should.

There's you, of course, as the founder and holder of the company vision. (Don't outsource yourself.) Maybe your business can thrive with you alone on the inside, but that's not always the case. So think carefully about what you choose to give to whom, and why.

Though conventional wisdom would say "core competencies"— whatever they may be in your particular industry—are what you keep in-house, I don't think that's always right. My company, for example, has built a reputation as a creative agency with the technical chops to integrate complex systems into digital experience platforms. It's one of our key business pillars, but I don't write a line of code myself, and neither do my direct hires: that's all handled by my outsourced team of elite developers.

What I and my in-house team members have in common is that we regularly interact with my company's clients and contractors. We're the front-of-house team, if you will.

That's not to say that my contractors never speak to my clients— many of them do—but client interactions are not a core company value I expect them to deliver. Their value instead is created more behind the scenes.

This is because client relations, for my company, are not simply a pass-through interface. We're not just relaying messages back and forth. We're doing all the work a creative agency does to understand our clients' needs and ambitions, to articulate their goals and clarify their visions. We're also collaborating with our contractors to understand what's possible, to see the opportunities to stretch beyond what our clients think they need.

Our greatest value comes from holding the vision and facilitating the conversations. So that's not something we can hand off to others.

But everything else? We outsource to contractors.

Baron uses contractors even more extensively than I do. Even key leaders of client strategy are veterans in their fields who prefer the flexibility of contract work at Carabiner to the commitments of a salaried position.

You'll make your own decisions about what can be handled by contractors and what can't. Make those decisions with care, and as Carabiner's example shows—an openness to entrusting even critical roles to superstar contractors.

Choose Partners Who are Invested in Their Businesses (No Side Hustlers Need Apply)

Contractors become contractors for many different reasons and in many different modes. For anyone you consider, evaluate where this work fits in their career journey so far.

Experience and exposure contractors are taking on contract work as a step along the way to something else. They're freelancing in hopes of landing full-time employment.

Fallback contractors are working as contractors because they lost or couldn't get a regular job. They're doing what they have to do, not what they want to do.

Side hustle contractors give most of their time and attention to something else. You are, at best, their second priority.

Career contractors choose the contractor lifestyle and invest in it as a business—and are the only kind of contractors you should hire.

They may have chosen this path because they like the flexibility it brings to work where they want and on their own schedule. Maybe they like being self-directed or have no patience for office politics. (This was certainly part of what drove me to strike out on my own.) Or maybe they've reached a level in their field where no one employer could afford to pay the full-time value of their work.

What's key is that they choose to be contractors, and they invest in the success of their practice. They aren't just selling off their time for dollars and hoping for the best. They want to grow, and they'll invest the effort of growing with you as long as you make it worth their while.

"It's not just about making money for them," Baron says. "Many have left corporate jobs where they had the ability to make more money. It's about fulfillment.

"One is a serial novelist, and she's gone on to write and publish several novels while working with us," he says. "Some like to walk their dogs in the afternoon. Some want to volunteer with their schools. Some want to travel more, and some want to travel less."

These personal motivations matter to Baron, and he enjoys being able to support what's important to the people with whom he partners. It also shows him where he and his contractors can come together in common cause.

"I look for capabilities, through referrals and reputation," he says. "But I also look for the genuineness of why they're doing what they're doing. My reason for doing it may be different from theirs, but it occupies the same space in our hearts. That creates a connection we can build on."

Share Your Vision

"Where there is no vision, the people perish," says Baron, paraphrasing Proverbs 29:18. "Where there is a vision, the people flourish."

Full-time employees don't become invested in your company's success just because you give them an employment contract, health insurance, and a regular paycheck. And the lack of those trappings is no impediment to contractors believing in you and therefore working hard to help you succeed.

"People can be loyal to a cause, a person," says Baron. "That person can be themselves. They can be loyal to quality."

When you share your vision with your contractors, you can inspire them to join you on your journey, no full-time employment required.

"If you're clear on where you're going," says Baron, "the superstars who join the party absorb it, and it becomes important to them too. They adopt the vision you espouse."

The rallying cry at my agency is "brands that work." We don't design pretty brands to win awards. We build what will help our clients succeed. We do this because it's what best serves our clients, but also because it's what I believe will best serve my agency's success.

Everyone on my team, contractors included, hears me talk about this regularly, both in the abstract and in the midst of every client project. They see my vision clearly, and they adopt it as their own, for the benefit of our clients, the growth of my agency, and the expansion of their own future opportunities.

Plug Them Into *Your* Systems

Your company is the nexus where client goals and contractor value comes together. You are the organizing principle, not anyone else.

As I explained in-depth in chapter 2, systems are the foundation of flexibility. Adapting your systems to the eccentricities of every contractor is therefore wildly inefficient.

Instead, standardize your systems for working with contractors. Design efficient, scalable systems for project management, client processes, communications, payment, and more—systems that are optimized for working with outside teams. Where you can, build in a degree of flexibility. Then insist that all your contractors plug into your system.

It's more efficient for everyone, and it's more effective too. You'll deliver better value to your clients, and that leads to better opportunities for your contractors.

Your clients will feel this integration, perhaps not consciously but palpably. Without it, clients will perceive your company as a loose confederation. With it, they'll experience a predictable, effective, and coordinated effort by a unified team of experts. The status of anyone's employment won't matter.

Show your contractors how they can hook into your interface, then forget about it and focus on delivering value to your clients.

Be Generous to Your Team

Transactional relationships are bad for business and worse for the soul. Your elastic team is critical to your small by design success. So show your gratitude and help them grow with you.

I think most people who choose to be small by design understand that we're not doing this just for overflowing bank accounts. We know there are easier paths to that.

Instead we want our work to be meaningful, and we want the same in our relationships.

"Expand your circle of people who you care about," Baron says. "Respect people different than you. Increase your feelings of care and compassion for them. You'll broaden the capability of your heart."

So don't treat your contractors like vending machines: putting in your money and taking out what you need. Build a real relationship, and give them more than just their fees.

As Baron does, find out what fulfills them, and how to support that. A cabin in the mountains for the novelist's next writing retreat. A company volunteer day at the parent's school. A donation in their name to the local dog shelter.

When a contractor delivers something exceptional that helps your business surge forward, give them a bonus.

Help them grow their own business, too. (Because, as I said earlier in this chapter, all the contractors you work with are making a career of contracting.) Refer clients to them when your company isn't the right fit. Write positive reviews of them on reputation sites. Give them some free advice or consulting that comes from your area of expertise. Pick up the phone or meet them for coffee if they're dealing with a challenge and could use your help.

Your contractors' growth and success will serve yours too. And the relationships you'll build together in the process will make all of it more fulfilling.

Celebrate Their (Other) Successes

Success is a duet you dance with your whole team.

Yes, you want your contractors to feel invested in your small by design business. But that investment should flow in both directions. You should also want every team member to grow and succeed, both with and beyond their partnership with you. Ultimately, their growth will serve yours too.

If a contractor calls you to share their excitement when they land a big new client, you're doing something right. (If they hide it, it's time for some self-reflection.)

Contractors, by definition and law, aren't beholden to work exclusively for you. They should use their skills to deliver value to other clients, even skills they honed working with you. It's how they will thrive.

Truly proprietary methods and information are a different matter, but you should define these boundaries at the beginning—narrowly and with precision. You didn't invent the idea that you should ask a client a bunch of questions at the start of a new project. If one of your contractors improves their discovery process as a result of working with you, great! And if they land better new clients as a result, even better! (Maybe they'll also refer some new clients to you.)

Go way beyond letting your contractors know it's okay to work with other clients. Celebrate their growth, their success. Send them a bottle of champagne or a box of cookies when they hit a major milestone in their own company's growth. Take them out to a fancy dinner or throw them a party.

Let them know you're happy for them and that you celebrate their success.

Pull Aside the Curtain to Show Them Your Business

Your small by design business shouldn't be a black box to your contractors. Let them see what's going on inside.

Trust your contractors enough to share what's going on with your business beyond the specific tasks you ask them to complete. (If you don't trust them enough to do this, you may need to reevaluate the contractors you're choosing.)

I do this all the time with my outsourced team of web developers. They've shared with me that most of their business growth has come directly from the growth of my own business, so we talk all the time about my plans for growth, and how they can support them.

I share with them:

- My goals for growth in the year ahead, and how I plan to pursue them.

- The general shape of the deals I'm presently trying to close, and the interesting challenges I'll be bringing their way once I do.
- The challenges that are hard right now, and what I'm trying to do better.

In showing your contractors what's behind the curtain at your company, you'll also reinforce the norm that they can give you the same transparency into their business.

It will mean they can tell you what they're struggling with before they blow the deadline, giving you an opportunity to work with them to solve the problem. Or they can share a growth goal they have that might align well with yours, opening up a new level of partnership and collaboration.

Contractors, if you choose the right ones, are business owners like you. You actually have a lot in common, and these conversations may be beneficial for both of you.

Get Them Invested in Your Shared Success

There's a world of difference between asking a contractor to do free work "for exposure," and inviting them to invest in your shared success.

Never ask a contractor to do free work that only benefits you. Instead, invite them to contribute to your mutual prosperity.

This must not be merely a semantic shift. Their investment must have the real potential of a payoff that makes the invested time worth their while, and you should make that payoff explicit along with any ask.

"We establish a Carabiner rate with everybody," says Baron. "If they spend any time at all on non-client work, we tell them to bill us for it.… Some won't bill us, and others do, but there is no expectation that they will do things for us for free. We always want to pay them for their time."

Pitching to a big potential client? Within a trusting relationship between you and your contractors, it's perfectly reasonable to invite their thinking for the proposal you're writing. You'll be surprised how often they won't charge you for that work.

They know you're invested in their success. And because of that, they're also invested in yours.

Be Loyal to Your Team

Once you find the right contractor for a particular capability your business needs, work with them exclusively and let them know you're doing so.

My contractors all understand they have first right of refusal on any job I have that matches their capabilities. (To this day, I haven't had one turn any work away.)

Different capabilities may require different contractors, but, wherever possible, seek to broaden their exclusive domain as you deepen the relationship.

Do you only go to the food photographer for food photography? Or are they also talented portrait photographers who you can turn to for headshots?

Does your front end developer regularly collaborate with a talented back end developer? Give them exclusivity as a package deal.

Wherever you can get quality results from a fewer number of trusted contractors, you should do so. It's more efficient for you and better supports your mutual success. So give them exclusivity for all that they can ably provide.

While one of the benefits of developing a team of contractors is the flexibility it gives you to cut costs quickly, you should do your best to take care of all your partners even when revenue slows.

"In tough times," says Baron, "we have no overhead, no payroll. We can thin things out and share the workload." But even when business is slow, he tries to give all the contractors on his team as much work and income as he can.

"Be there for them when times are tough," he says. "Be willing to take a hit financially, making sure the people you care about don't suffer."

Your transparency and vision will help during hard times too. Give your partners the information they need to pivot and prepare, all the support you're able to provide, and a reason to stick with you for the better days ahead.

Carabiner Adapts to a Crisis

When the COVID-19 pandemic hit in early 2020, Carabiner lost some business. It was in many ways reminiscent of the dotcom bubble burst 20 years earlier. World events were causing a macroeconomic crisis, threatening the health of Baron's business.

Baron and his elastic team at Carabiner were ready.

This time, there was no office space lease to manage, and barely any fixed overhead. Revenue was down, but most costs were tied directly to revenue streams. With less work coming in, Carabiner was paying contractors less too, though out of both loyalty and generosity, Baron did spread around as much work as he could to each.

As veteran contractors, they were all savvy entrepreneurs themselves. They made good money in the company's busier times and were prepared for the occasional stretch of lean months.

Meanwhile, Baron was transparent with everyone about the loss of business, and about his plans to restore health and prosperity to Carabiner. He also invited them, on a purely volunteer basis, to leverage their own networks to generate new business for the company.

"Let's reach out to people we know," he said. "If you're interested in doing this we'll circle up once a week and have a 15-minute chat about who we're reaching out to."

Several contractors took him up on the invitation. Others didn't, and that was fine with Baron too. He understood that, as entrepreneurs themselves, each needed to adjust in their own way. He was as flexible with them as he asked them to be with him.

Because of Carabiner's own business development efforts, their elastic playbook for working with contractors, and the macroeconomic recovery, business was soon growing strongly again, to the benefit of everyone—contractors most definitely included.

As we've seen in the last few chapters, your small by design business can make a major impact. The secret to sustaining such results—and the greatest satisfaction too—is in the relationships you develop and deepen through your work. I'll talk more about those relationships in the next section.

SECTION THREE:

Relationships by Design

Chapter 7:

DON'T BE AFRAID TO SAY NO, DON'T BE AFRAID TO SAY YES

Saying Yes (and No) Takes MEPTIK to New York

From a trade show projection to a pop-up store in New York, Sarah Linebaugh was strategic about her yeses and nos as she developed a relationship with a major skincare brand, a partnership that helped both businesses grow.

Linebaugh is the co-founder and creative director of MEPTIK, a nine-person, Atlanta-based studio specializing in experiential design and virtual production. Their client list has included Home Depot, AT&T, and Drunk Elephant, at the time the number one skincare brand at Sephora.

"Drunk Elephant found us on Instagram and approached us to design projection mapping content for a Sephora trade show booth," says Linebaugh.

Even though this was a major, organic win for her, over the next several years, Linebaugh was thoughtful and deliberate about when she said yes to opportunities offered by Drunk Elephant and when she said no. Her careful decisions helped develop a strong and enduring relationship with the brand.

Curation is Key

Warren Buffet famously said, "The difference between successful people and really successful people is that really successful people say no to almost everything."

I won't try to improve on the Sage of Omaha, but I do want to point out the heightened importance of carefully curating the projects you accept when your company is small by design.

This idea is driven partly by a limit of capacity. Small businesses can only take on so many projects at one time without sacrificing sleep, sanity, relationships, quality, or all four. But it's also because, when you're small, every single project tells the story of who you are. (Refer back to chapter 4 for more on that.)

When you're first getting your business up and running, you may find yourself saying yes to just about any opportunity that comes your way. That may be necessary in the beginning as you hustle to pay the bills while establishing your niche, but, as I discussed in chapter 3, it's not a strategy for sustainable abundance.

In his book, Traction: Get a Grip on Your Business, Gino Wickman makes this same point when he says, "This helter-skelter method may have gotten you to where you are today and helped you survive the early drought, but to break through the ceiling, you have to create some focus."

When you're offered projects or clients that exceed your capacity or tell the wrong story, don't be afraid to say no.

But that doesn't mean you have to turn down every project that isn't a perfect fit. Too-small projects can lead to bigger opportunities. Less familiar fields can become new specialties. Staffing shortages can be filled with capable contractors. (Refer back to chapter 6 for more on that.)

What I'm saying is, even if a potential project or client makes you a little bit nervous, don't be afraid to say yes.

The key is carefully curating the projects you accept, and setting yourself up for success.

Don't Just Go With Your Gut

There's a tendency in business to glorify decisiveness in a leader, over looking the importance of the deliberation that precedes it. We like leaders who shoot from the hip, go with their gut, make the call, and never look back.

I don't think that's the right approach for a small by design business. Design implies deliberation, intention, and thoughtful decisions.

A small by design business also doesn't ask you to make dozens of immediate, critical decisions every day, as a leader of a large corporation may be required to do. Instead your clients and projects are comparatively few, and you can delegate many tactical decisions to your team.

When you're small by design, you have the luxury of taking the time to make all your important decisions with care. (Any potential client who demands an immediate answer is probably not someone you want to work with.) So whenever a new opportunity comes your way, consider it from several angles to decide whether it's the right opportunity for you.

Here are some of the principles that guide me, Linebaugh, and other small by design businesses as we decide when to say yes and when to say no.

A Playbook for Yes and No

Start Small Then Go Deep

If you're a small by design company, Fortune 500 clients may not give you that $10 million dream contract on your very first engagement. So don't be afraid to say yes to a "get to know you" project if you can both see clear value ahead.

Will this new project give you an opportunity to develop reference-quality work (see chapter 4)? Will it open up opportunities to build a lasting relationship with the client? Then don't be afraid to say yes.. as long as you can do the job well.

In order to go deep with the client, always offer more value than they request. Then, if you have an opportunity to bid on or propose additional projects, be ready to surpass with the sequel.

Don't wait for these "smart small" clients to ask for more. Propose solutions that fulfill all their requirements, then suggest how you could deliver even more value than they imagined. Return to them with even bigger and better ideas. They'll soon be saying yes to the contracts of your dreams, the opportunities that will be a resounding yes for you.

That's what MEPTIK did for Drunk Elephant.

The skincare brand was preparing to showcase their new products to Sephora employees at an annual internal trade show. After being Instagram-astounded, they came to Linebaugh to design projection mapping content for their booth. The request was well within MEP-TIK's capabilities, so it was easy to say yes to this opportunity, but Linebaugh went one better, suggesting real-time interactive graphics.

"The theme was 'Acid Trip,' because their products have healthy acids for your skin," says Linebaugh. "They wanted this whole seventies vibe, so we created these acidy swirls that you could control with your gestures. There were lips that would blow you kisses when you touched them. And there were letters that you could wave your hand at, and they would highlight keywords related to the product. It all made their graphics a lot more engaging than they would have been otherwise."

The "Acid Trip" interactive experience was a hit at the trade show. Drunk Elephant learned that MEPTIK brought more than great execution to the table; they also brought great new ideas. So for the next trade show, they came back to Linebaugh for more.

Be Sure of Your Brainpower

You don't have to know how to do everything the project will require. Anything worth doing will push you and your team to learn something new. But you do have to investigate the requirements and honestly assess whether you and your team know enough to figure out the rest and deliver quality results on schedule. (Doing so certainly helped Linebaugh when a second Drunk Elephant opportunity came along.)

Tangential in-house knowledge counts if you know it can be directly applied. For example, my agency has developed ecommerce sites using several online ordering platforms. If a new project comes along that requires us to use an online ordering platform not familiar to us, we have a high degree of confidence we can figure it out. So we're not afraid to say yes.

It's also okay to rely on contractors and partners for some of the needed brainpower (see chapter 6), as long as someone on your in-house team understands the topic well enough to manage the work and handle quality control.

For the next Sephora trade show, the people at Drunk Elephant came back to MEPTIK, asking, "Why don't you design the whole booth rather than just the content?"

Linebaugh knew that the expanded scope would extend beyond her team's core competency of creating digital environments, rather than building physical ones. But she had previously collaborated with fabricators on similar projects, and she had a contractor in place whom she could trust. Not all the needed brainpower was employed by her company, but she knew where she would get it. So she said yes to the job.

"Fake it 'til you make it," the advice often goes, but that's actually pretty awful advice. When you deliver on what you promise to your clients (and then deliver more), you earn their trust and build a long-term relationship. If you fail to provide because you took on something beyond your team's current brainpower, you could lose that trust (and that client) forever. So Linebaugh made sure she and her team were equipped to create a magical experience—in more ways than one.

"[Drunk Elephant] came to us with a 'Genie in the Bottle' theme, inspired by the 'I Dream of Jeannie' TV show of the 1960s," she says. "So we shaped the whole booth like a bottle. We had our fabricator make a replica of Jeannie's couch, and we reproduced the patterns on her walls."

With a truly unique structure as their canvas, and a trusted outside partner to handle fabrication, the MEPTIK team created an immersive, interactive digital experience that used facial tracking and digital genies to engage with passersby. Drunk Elephant was once again delighted.

Consequently, they started asking MEPTIK to handle more of their trade show booths, and, when an even bigger opportunity came along, MEPTIK was the obvious choice.

Know Where You'll Get the People Power

While one person's good idea can transform a client's trajectory, the implementation of some ideas requires the work of many hands. Brains alone aren't always enough; sometimes you need more bodies too. This is one scenario in which your small by design company may struggle with a staffing limitation that large companies don't have. Who will you turn to for help?

Be realistic about your capacity. Do you truly have enough available people on your team to do the job? For a small by design company, the answer is often no, but that's not necessarily a big deal. As I discussed in chapter 6, contractors can give you the elasticity you need to expand your workforce at need.

In order to say yes with confidence, ask whether your existing network of contractors has all the people you need to serve your client well, and whether they're properly integrated into your team to deliver quality results. If not, what's your plan for expanding that network without sacrificing quality? Don't know? This might be a good time to say no.

As Drunk Elephant grew into a major international brand, and on the heels of the successful "Genie in a Bottle" booth project, they came to Linebaugh with an opportunity to help design a pop-up store in New York City. It was in many ways a dream project for MEPTIK. They would take on responsibility for helping to design and fabricate an entire in-store experience, from projection mapping and digital interaction to shelves, counters, and lighting.

"It was the biggest project that we had ever been offered at that point in time," says Linebaugh, "so we really wanted to take on the whole thing."

But there was a problem: Linebaugh was due to give birth to her first child two weeks before the pop-up was to go live. Her co-founder and CTO, Nicholas Rivero, is also her husband. MEPTIK's two principal officers would be going through one of the greatest transitions in their family life right when their team would need them to deliver on the most demanding project in the company's history.

After careful consideration and many conversations with her husband and her team, Linebaugh said yes to the digital experiential design component of the project, but no to the rest of the physical store's fabrication. Because of the solid relationship and trust they'd already established, Drunk Elephant agreed to work with their own contract designer and fabricator to handle the portion that MEPTIK couldn't.

It was a hard decision for Linebaugh, but one she has never regretted. Even with the reduced scope on her end, the pop-up store stretched MEPTIK's team to their limits. But they were able to deliver the quality experience that Drunk Elephant had come to expect of them, in ways they couldn't have if they hadn't said no to a portion of the ask.

Because they carefully considered their capacity before committing, then went on to deliver quality results for Drunk Elephant, MEPTIK has since had opportunities with other clients to take on projects just as ambitious—without the added stress of pregnancy, childbirth, and the early weeks of raising a newborn baby.

Say Yes (or No) to Small Pilot Projects

When you run a small by design business, you have the freedom to explore projects outside your current focus and expertise, as long as you do so with a plan for serving these clients (and your own story) well.

My agency sometimes bids on projects that are tangential to our existing specialties. If the opportunity is in an area that I think could potentially become a new vertical for my company—one well aligned with our story—then I consider several questions:

- **Is the project small enough?** Don't take on large contracts as pilot projects. If your team hates the work or struggles to deliver, you could be in for a long haul of stress and misery. Minimize the potential downside by only pursuing opportunities that are short-term and small.
- **Can we learn this?** As I said above about brainpower, it's okay not to know everything at the beginning. Pilot projects are, by definition, times when you don't already know all you need to know. But research the requirements enough to assess whether you and your team can figure it out on schedule.
- **Will we have enough time?** And about that schedule—Don't accept rush jobs or tight deadlines if you're learning something new. You and your team need time to learn and explore. Rush jobs are for areas in which you're already experts.
- **Is there enough opportunity to make it worth our while?** You probably won't make major profits on a pilot project. You'll spend extra time learning, and you'll have to develop new systems for efficient delivery. Breaking even is just fine, as long as there's the potential for this to become a profitable new vertical. If there isn't, then it's not an exploration that's worth your time.
- **Are we really interested?** Are you running a pilot project because you really don't know? Or because you're not interested but are afraid to say no to the opportunity? If it's anywhere close to the latter, just say no.

A few years ago, I accepted an invitation to bid on a project for The Coca-Cola Company, building out educational content for internal use on a leading e-learning platform—one we had never developed on before. It was an opportunity to experiment with something new, so I considered all the questions above.

The initial project was small, and the timeline was reasonable. I researched the platform enough to know we could figure it out, and I knew that Coca-Cola had a substantial ongoing need for more e-learning development. The money was good, and I liked the idea of having the company in my portfolio. I also knew doing well with this might lead to other opportunities with the company.

I said yes. We did the work, and the client was happy with the results.

We also learned that we never wanted to develop on this e-learning platform again. The work was far too mechanical, with little room for creativity. We didn't have any fun. When Coca-Cola asked us to do more, we said no.

I don't regret the initial yes. The pilot project served its purpose. It taught us that we didn't enjoy this kind of work. While we enjoyed the people at Coca-Cola and would gladly work with them again, we now know that any future opportunities to develop on this e-learning platform will be a no.

In contrast, when a state university came to us for help with website accessibility remediation, following a finding that they were in violation of the Americans with Disabilities Act (ADA), we weren't yet website accessibility experts, but I was immediately interested in the idea.

We took the project on as an experiment, and my team was very inspired by the work. They soon became experts in accessible website design and development, and champions of its importance.

That yes shifted my company in some fundamental ways. Accessibility became one of our core values, giving me and my team an added sense of purpose in our work. And it opened up many future opportunities for us, with both existing clients and new.

We now build best practices for website accessibility into every web design project we accept. It's non-negotiable. I write and speak extensively on website accessibility, and it has brought lots of new business our way, work that we feel really good about doing. For us, website accessibility work is now an easy yes.

So don't be afraid to say yes (or no) to a small experiment. It could have impacts both lasting and large.

Refer When You're Not the Right Fit

When deciding whether to say yes or no, consider if someone else in your network can do the project better than you. I'm not talking about a direct competitor, but rather someone in a specialty adjacent to your own.

My agency can manage social media campaigns, but not as well as Imagine Media (featured in chapter 5), which specializes in this area.

We can design and build simple, templatized websites for businesses without the budget for the custom work we usually do. But I know another web development agency that specializes in sites like these, building them well on a tight budget, with speed and efficiency.

I've cultivated many wonderful relationships with other talented small by design businesses. So when an opportunity comes my way that I know is a better fit for someone else, I'm never afraid to say, "No, this is not a good fit, but I know someone else who can help."

I'd rather refer these opportunities than try to contort my company to provide what they need. Because these services aren't our central focus, we haven't built the systems to deliver quality with efficiency. Taking on two simple social media clients would crush my team more than completing two complex online ordering platforms, because we already have our systems in place for the latter.

Also, as I'll talk about more in chapter 9, it's deeply satisfying for me to support other small by design companies in my network. And of course I know they'll reciprocate with opportunities that are a better fit for me.

I want the referrals I make to be appropriate, warmly received, and successful for both parties. So when I decide to shift an opportunity to someone else, I never just forward along an email or share a URL. Yes, we business owners are busy people. But there is real value in giving a little of your time to these clients, even when you know you're going to turn down the project.

In cases like these, I get on the phone with the client, investing 30 to 60 minutes to gain a real sense of who they are and what they need. I explain to them what my company does, then tell them why I want to recommend them to someone else.

"We're not going to be able to do as good a job for you as this other team," I might say. "This isn't our core competency, but it is theirs."

Then I introduce them to the other company with a well-informed explanation of what the client needs.

I do the same for existing clients when they come to me with an opportunity to expand the scope of our contract. After assessing our own capacity, if I know someone else in our network can serve this particular need better, I refer them.

The time and effort I put into these warm and informed referrals is worth it to me if it leads to another great team in my network getting a good project. It's also an investment in the reciprocal leads I know these connections may send my way.

Never be afraid to say no to a potential client, but, when you can, refer them to someone who will give them a better yes.

Prioritize Passion and Satisfaction

One of the great joys of staying small by design is the freedom it gives you to forego volume for fulfillment. This is where you may come closest to going with your gut.

A potential project can look great on paper. It can check all the analytical boxes and serve your revenue goals. Yet still you may want to say no, simply because you know it won't bring you any deeper satisfaction. It won't inspire your team. It won't give you opportunities to develop new skills.

For instance, I'll never again take another e-learning course building project, even though I now know we can do the work well and receive good payment for it. There's just no happiness in it for me and my team. We don't enjoy the work, and it doesn't help us grow. Because we said yes to a small experiment, I now will always say no.

In contrast, my team is passionate about accessible web design. It aligns with our values, and we care deeply about the work. So when a potential client comes to me wanting to invest in a more accessible website, I'll usually say yes.

At MEPTIK, Linebaugh often asks her team's opinion when considering a new project. "Do we want to take this on? Is this project going to be fun for everybody?"

Staying small by design allows MEPTIK to factor joy into every project decision. Small by design can do the same for you.

"That's one advantage of being on a small team," says Linebaugh. "We can take stock a little easier than larger companies of how our team is feeling. We can make sure that we are all working on things that we enjoy."

Passion is why Linebaugh and her husband started the company, and staying small by design allows them to stay true to that.

"I've always been passionate about the creative side," she says. "My partner has always been passionate about the technical. And we just wanted to do cool stuff. That was always our driving factor. We've got these skills. We love working on new and exciting things that combine creativity and technology. So whatever allows us to use our skills in different, exciting ways: that's the driving force behind what we've done."

Prioritizing their own passion, the people of MEPTIK enjoy their work more. And that joy helps them create more joyful experiences for their audiences.

Sidebar: On Saying Yes Because You Need the Money

One of the benefits of staying small by design is keeping your fixed costs low. With responsible financial planning, you shouldn't need a lot of revenue just to keep the lights on. (Rent someone else's lights on an as-needed basis instead.)

Make the most of this freedom by avoiding saying yes to projects just because you need the money. (And refer back to chapter 3 to develop financial systems that won't put you in such a bind to begin with.)

I once said yes to a client because I thought we needed the revenue to pay the bills. I knew the project wasn't right for us, nor was the client. But I didn't know where else the money would come from if I didn't say yes to the bad opportunity in front of my face. I was afraid to say no.

As I had plenty of reason to expect from the beginning, the relationship with the client was acrimonious and only got worse. The project wasn't interesting or in any way rewarding to me or my team. And shortly after I accepted the project, we won another contract that was far more interesting, covering all our revenue needs for months to come.

Because I'd made a decision driven by financial fear, we were all stuck working on a project we didn't care about, with a client we didn't like, for money we no longer needed. I'd committed to delivering, and we did so. But I was never happier than when the client let us know that no further services would be required from us.

My only regret was that I ever said yes.

But let's be real: sometimes you will say yes because you need the money, especially when you're starting out. As I discussed in chapters 3 and 4, you may sometimes take on projects that aren't a perfect fit. That's okay, but, when you do, it's critical to know that's what you're doing, and you should make this abundantly clear to your team.

Maintain your quality standards, and do what you promise these clients you will do. But this isn't the time to overdeliver. These are projects you take for the immediate profit they'll bring, so control your costs with care and lean on your established systems to stay efficient.

Then use the profits from these projects to invest in a future for your company that won't require such compromises, so that next time you won't be afraid to say no.

Saying Yes Leads to a Deeper Understanding of MEPTIK's Drive

As it did for many companies, the COVID-19 pandemic forced a pivot on MEPTIK. Around the world, live events were postponed indefinitely or canceled outright. While MEPTIK has always created digital content, it was previously designed to be experienced in-person, not through the same screens we all lived and worked through during social distancing.

To keep the company's revenue flowing, MEPTIK turned to virtual film production. This cutting edge approach to filmmaking uses a game engine platform to bring live action film techniques to fully rendered virtual reality environments. It's the process behind the immersive world building in the 2019 remake of "The Lion King," as well as the HBO series "The Mandalorian" and several Phase Four television series in the Marvel Cinematic Universe.

"A lot of it is really similar to technology we were working with before," says Linebaugh, "but it's definitely a new field for us. Film production is not something we really had a background in, since we were more focused on live events, but we knew we could figure it out. It's different content, but a similar workflow to what we do for events, and I think we've adapted really well."

MEPTIK has become well known and respected for its virtual production work, and they saw their business not only survive but actually grow during the pandemic. The opportunities seem enormous, and it's interesting work too.

"It has been a really exciting season," says Linebaugh, "because it's pushed us into the cutting edge of a lot of technology and workflows that people are starting to use across the board from Marvel and huge action films, all the way to small commercials. We're riding this new wave of the film industry."

The pivot has honed MEPTIK's business with a deeper understanding of their core competencies and interests: real-time content and technical implementation.

"We have really begun to dial in what we're passionate about, and that's real-time content—for use in both experiential design and virtual film production," says Linebaugh. "We use similar workflows for both, whether we're creating touch-reactive visuals for a tradeshow booth or creating a CG scenic backdrop for a music video. Creating visuals that respond in real-time and implementing the technical back-end to bring them to life has always been what drives us, and it will continue to do so."

When Linebaugh first said yes to virtual film production, she did so with due deliberation and care, but there was no guarantee that MEPTIK's new direction would succeed. She said yes anyway, with an openness to new opportunities, confidence in her team's abilities, resources for when she needed help... and little fear.

When you have a company that's small by design, you don't have to be afraid to say no, and you don't have to be afraid to say yes.

The structures and stability of small by design give you the freedom and flexibility to consider new opportunities with confidence and integrity. They allow you to consider:

- Can you do the work?
- Do you want to?
- Will the outcome be meaningful to you?
- Will your team be passionate about the work?
- Will it help you all grow?
- Will it enhance the story of your company?

Ask all the questions that are important to you. Consider the values on which your business is built. Then make a decision—yes or no—and, either way, don't be afraid.

If you do say yes, then, as soon as you begin, set yourself up for success by preparing your clients to sell your best work. I'll explain what I mean by that in chapter 8.

Chapter 8:

TURN YOUR CLIENTS INTO SALESPEOPLE

Remaking Rumbling Bald

North Carolina lake community Rumbling Bald began with a solitary boathouse on Lake Lure, in the Blue Ridge Mountains. It's an area rich in history, including the Carolina Gold Rush of the 1800s, and its lush mountains and deep waters are the setting for films including "Firestarter," "Dirty Dancing," and "Last of the Mohicans."

Around this lake, an idyllic lakeside resort community has grown, with a blend of permanent residents, vacation homeowners, and visiting guests who come to swim and boat, hike and golf, rest and play, dine well, get married, celebrate reunions or birthdays, and generally live their lives in the midst of exquisite natural beauty.

Several years ago, Jeff Geisler, the general manager of Rumbling Bald (and formerly with Toyota before switching to the hospitality industry), approached my agency for assistance. The community was in many ways thriving, but their branding had not kept pace with their evolution, their values, or their vision for what the future might bring. Geisler asked us to help him rebrand the community.

"Our species is too enamored with transient things," says Geisler. "We wanted to pivot our brand to the underlying beauty of this place, and what that wakes up in people."

My agency hadn't worked previously in the hospitality industry, but it was an area that interested me and several members of my team. (The prospect of a discovery process that included complimentary stays in such a beautiful retreat was also an attractive bonus.) And though the initial project size was modest, I saw the potential to grow it into something more. So we said yes to the contract.

What followed were a series of interesting challenges, many of which had very little to do with brand development or execution, and everything to do with navigating the diverse priorities of people— including those outside of Geisler's team who had influence on the decisions. Our solution? Prepare and empower Geisler to sell our best ideas to his stakeholders.

The People You Never Meet Can Kill Your Best Ideas

This chapter is not necessarily about turning your clients into evangelists for your prospects with other companies, though that's certainly valuable to any small by design company. Instead it's about something subtler but so important in the B2B service world: helping your clients sell your best work for you within their organizations.

Let's face it: the innovative ideas that your point of contact loves often get derailed because another key stakeholder who you've never met doesn't get it or just really has never liked the color orange.

I'm not talking about situations where agencies push self-indulgent conceptual flourishes that feed their own egos and help them win awards. I'm talking about your groundbreaking ideas that are well aligned with a client's goals and identity. Daring approaches that your best research and expertise tell you will indeed be effective, if only everyone involved believes in you enough to step outside their comfort zones.

"One of the difficulties of any major change," says Geisler, "is the resistance of the status quo."

Stakeholder rejections are costly. Endless rounds of revisions, rework, redos, and change orders are inefficient and tend to lower your profit margins while watering down the work. There's an opportunity cost too. Think of all the precious time you could open up if clients bought into your ideas during the first round.

Remember the "reference quality work" Brad White talked about in chapter 4? Many a golden opportunity to produce such brand-defining work dies at the hands of stakeholders not sold on your vision.

Having your best ideas rejected isn't just bad for business. It's incredibly frustrating too, and it can make the work less satisfying for you and your team. There's a hidden cost to that. When your employees and contractors feel misunderstood and underappreciated, they're less likely to give you their best.

As business services entrepreneurs, we want more than to trade our work for dollars. Most of us want to serve our clients well with our most impactful ideas, and we take great pride in those projects where clients let us do our very best work. Bank deposits don't make up for the disappointment of good ideas denied approval in favor of mediocre alternatives.

"You're not just trying to sell something," says Geisler. "You want to sell something you're proud of and have it come to life. Not just some bastardized version that some committee gave you after they've beaten it up for three weeks."

When scenarios like this arise (and trust me, they will), it may be tempting to retreat to a cynical place and gripe about how clients "just don't get us," but I urge you not to go there. It becomes a self-fulfilling prophecy that saps the joy from your work.

Instead, consider that your clients don't get your ideas… yet. They will once you prepare your points of contact to sell.

Nemawashi and the Practice of Preparing the Ground

"Nemawashi is a Japanese gardening term," says Geisler, "and it encapsulates a major difference in approach that I saw in my business career prior to this, between Toyota and General Motors."

The core concept in nemawashi is that you must prepare the ground before making a big change.

"In Japan, if somebody wants to move a tree," says Geisler, "they take a quarter of the dirt from where the tree is, and move it to where the tree is going to be. And they take the dirt from where the tree is going to be to where the tree is. They do that once per season until they've completed a full year cycle. And so when they pick up the tree and move it, there's no shock to the tree. The tree knows what to expect. It's successful almost all the time."

In Japanese business culture, this concept has been applied to preparing the way for any major change. The principles of nemawashi say you must consult stakeholders before any significant decisions are made or announced. Invite their feedback and input from the beginning. Show them that their opinions are important and heard. Ask for their support.

Preparing the ground for change in this way doesn't happen quickly. It takes a lot of patience and intention. But if you do it well, the change, when its leaves unfurl, feels obvious, inevitable, and right.

Sell Your Big Idea (and the Next, and the Next...)

As I discussed in chapter 3, the cost of securing sales with new clients can be high, and that cost mostly falls on you as the founder. As I'll discuss more fully later in this chapter, it's far more efficient to expand your relationships with your existing clients, maximizing the value you deliver and earn from them.

So from the beginning of your first project with a new client, you should already be thinking about the next one you want to do with them… and the work you'll do together five years from now. This first project will set the trajectory for the future.

If you botch your introductory deal, there won't be a second one to follow. If you do good work without stakeholder buy-in, you might get another chance, but you'll have to hustle even harder. But if you do good work and also get enthusiastic stakeholder engagement, you'll be well on your way to a successful and sustainable long-term relationship with the client. As more decision makers become invested in the work you're doing, your point of contact will also find it easier to get approval each time they go asking for an increased budget to bring you back.

"It's easy to sell something," says Geisler, "when [what's being sold] represents a deep understanding of where you are and where you're trying to go."

I'll say more on that later, but for now, note that selling becomes easier once stakeholder trust and enthusiasm is established. Projects go more smoothly, with fewer roadblocks and a greater ability to deliver high-impact results.

When you help your point of contact successfully sell and deliver your projects to their stakeholders, you also help them become a hero, while you work quietly in the wings to support them: the Alfred to their Batman, the J.A.R.V.I.S. to their Iron Man. (This is as it should be.) They'll win, and will want to keep winning, so they'll keep coming back to you.

But all of this depends on being able to get your initial proposal approved.

The Importance of Prepping Your Points of Contact to Sell

In any organization larger than a single proprietorship, there are layers of decision makers with veto power over your work. It's critical to find out who they are, and, from day one of a new project, figure out how you'll sell them on your best ideas.

Fortunately or unfortunately, you often won't be in the meetings where your concepts are presented to these stakeholders. At some point, the sale has to come from within the organization. So it'll be all on your client to represent your work, explain your thinking, and make the case for why all the decision makers should approve it.

However, your point of contact may or may not be an expert in your field. If they're a CMO and you're a marketing agency, they probably have a good handle on your professional expertise. But what if they run a music festival and you're a web development firm? Or, as with Rumbling Bald, they're a general manager of a residential resort community and you're a branding agency?

Further: even if your client likes your ideas, can they explain why? Do they see your subtle strategies at play? Can they articulate them well to other audiences?

Even very smart people who are very good at what they do may not see what you see in the approach you propose to take. What may seem obvious to you may be mysterious to someone else. This is, after all, why you're the expert they hired. But to move forward, you have to help them see it, then help them present it well.

Preparing your point of contact to sell your concepts is the difference between getting 80 to 90% of your best, boldest ideas approved and maybe only 50%. It can also make the difference between a one-off project and a long-time partner who returns to you again and again.

Here's how you can get the greenlight from stakeholders at the get-go for even your most audacious approaches.

A Playbook for Prepping Your Clients to Sell

Know All Your Audiences

As I discussed above, in order to help your client sell your concept, you first have to know who the stakeholders and decision-making influencers are—from the very beginning of the project.

I'm not only talking here about the chain of command: your point of contact's boss, boss' boss, and so on. Where you find stakeholders will vary from client to client based on their industry and structure. Is there a board of directors? A body of longtime donors? Are the leads at other divisions involved? Will local government have a say? Might even some key customers be part of the conversation?

Ask your client who else in the organization's hierarchy will weigh in on your ideas. Ask also if there is a broader community whose opinions will be influential. Keep asking until you're confident you have the full list.

Include these people in your discovery process from day one if you can. Invite them into your initial workshops, interview them, or send them a questionnaire. Ask about their goals, values, and priorities.

This is about more than putting a good sales spin on whatever you want to do. Instead, take what you learn from everyone in the discovery process, and genuinely reflect their opinions and priorities in the work. Make sure they feel authentically involved and heard.

My agency once did a rebrand and new digital experience platform (DXP) for an agricultural, state-funded Georgia college founded in 1908. Our client was the college's CIO. Students were the primary audience, though they wouldn't ultimately make the final decisions.

We soon learned however, that the people who cared most about the brand were the local residents of the town, many of them graduates who stayed to build their lives there and had a deep, emotional connection to the university. They saw it as the foundation and cultural center of their town.

We knew we had to celebrate the college's long history while evolving its brand to work better in the digital age. So we visited the archives in the school's library, scanning yearbooks, farmer's guides from the '40s, and newspapers from throughout the college's history. This research all informed the new brand.

To prepare the CIO to present the brand, we developed a presentation deck that included some of the scanned archival material, plus talking points explaining how the college's history had inspired the new brand. For example, the new font was ADA-compliant, legible at small sizes, and had a flexible webfont available. But the community residents wouldn't care about that. Instead, we pointed out that the font was created the same year as the college, and we included scans of century-old print materials that had used it.

Before presenting to the university's president, the CIO took a printout of our brand proposal and walked it down to the local diner during breakfast time—to test how our concept might land with stakeholders who wouldn't actually be at the meeting. He showed it to the restaurant owner and several of the patrons. (The next time we visited him, the printout was tattered and smelled like pancakes.) They got it, they liked it, and he knew then that the brand would be a success.

Because he took this extra step of nemawashi to get audience buy-in, the brand was ultimately approved. Five years later, we're still working with them on additional modernizations of their website.

Similarly, when Geisler came to us for the Rumbling Bald rebrand, we knew the property owners association (POA) would be a very important stakeholder. He and his team wanted a brand that would attract more vacationers and buyers to the resort, but he needed the support of the current homeowners. So we included them in our discovery workshops. We asked for their input and got their buy-in on the long-term goals the new brand would support.

"It wasn't forced," says Geisler. "It wasn't, 'Here's the answer we want to get from you all.' It was organic. By going through that process, we realized that we had a lot of common desires. There was a sense at a point in the meeting where we realized, okay, we're really all on the same page."

Based on what all stakeholders (including homeowners) said in the discovery workshops, we drafted a Rumbling Bald purpose and promise, then turned that into a manifesto—one that spoke to the values and vision of the homeowners as well as the resort management.

We didn't move forward with creating the brand until everyone agreed on the manifesto and the goals it implied.

By taking time early on to understand the crucial audiences—even the ones who may not seem immediately obvious—you'll create work you know will speak to them, and therefore will sell well.

Help Them See What You See

As a professional in your field, you see things in your work that most people don't. There's a strategy and structure to what you're proposing: a craft and creativity. This involves both lessons of education and experience, and natural talent and intuition.

When you present your ideas to your point of contact, you probably help them understand your thinking, but the moment you hand off your thoughts (no matter how precise you've been), you're in a game of telephone, making it harder for them to deliver your message to the next listener: their stakeholders.

So do everything you can to help them see your work as clearly as you do. Point out how you applied not only their ideas, but the ideas of the stakeholders who you consulted during your discovery: "In the workshop, you said you wanted our new brand to _____, and that's why the agency chose _____." Or, to take an example from Ron Perry, who I talked about in chapter 1: "You said we need to balance slip prevention with sanitation, and that's why the contractor used this floor material."

Go the extra mile with helpful presentation materials. Equip your client with mock-ups that bring the proposed experience to life.

To illustrate: As the time approached for Geisler to present the new brand to the Rumbling Bald POA, we sent a photographer to capture beautiful images of the community, including all existing signage. We edited these photos, inserting our new designs to show how the proposed new brand would actually look in their community. These were included in a presentation deck with talking points that referenced the goals they had all agreed upon together.

As a result, when Geisler presented everything to the POA, they all saw it clearly.

When you help your own points of contact see what you see, you empower them to share that vision with their stakeholders and sell your ideas well.

Further Prepare the Client to Sell

Think about all the preparation and practice you put into presenting a proposal to a potential client. Great ideas are fundamental, but they rarely sell themselves. You know this, and it's why you put in the work to present them well.

Your client should do no less when presenting to stakeholders, and you should help prepare them, just as you would prepare yourself.

One powerful way to do this is to script their presentation or give them talking points, as best suits their speaking style. Prepare a slide deck or other audio-visual aids. As we did with Rumbling Bald, print or produce photographs, scale models, brochures, or whatever will make the presentation more compelling.

But also keep it real. Your clients will present most effectively when they're genuinely passionate about what they're saying. Build their presentation around their authentic enthusiasm, not what's most interesting to you.

Then rehearse and revise. Ask your clients to practice presenting the work to your team, so they'll feel more at ease later when they do so with their stakeholders. Observing them in rehearsal, you'll be able to identify which ideas they articulate with authenticity and ease. Edit out anything that sounds forced or false.

Above all, give them a presentation they can deliver with natural and heartfelt enthusiasm.

To show how this works: my company once launched a major rebrand of a Jewish music festival. The organization had expanded its mission to include the intersection of Jewish music and culture with the other music and cultures of the South. The executive director wanted a new name and brand to reflect this shift.

But their fiscal stability relied on legacy donors who had supported the organization as they'd known it for more than a decade. The new brand couldn't alienate these supporters. Donors wouldn't be sold by promises of better conversion rates, because their motivations were emotional. So we prepared the executive director to tell a stirring story about the history of the organization and how they were passing the torch to this new generation.

We had him practice presenting to us, and we took note of where he seemed either awkward or at ease. He even called some of these beats out to us, saying, "This phrasing doesn't feel comfortable. Can you help me reword this so it feels more like me?"

For points that seemed harder for him to present, we didn't coach him. Instead, we revised until they flowed naturally from his authentic passion.

The entire presentation was based on his emotion and how people perceived his own confidence in the proposed changes. Presenting with genuine passion, he successfully sold his stakeholders on the new name and brand.

When the updated brand launched, legacy donors remained loyal to the organization, while the expanded vision drew in additional first-time support. With a cool and hip new name and brand, they were able to attract fresh sponsors and book musical acts who had been previously out of their reach. Influential music publications started paying attention too, bringing the festival into a larger national conversation.

None of this would have happened if the executive director hadn't successfully sold a daring rebrand to his stakeholders.

Similarly, before Geisler presented the Rumbling Bald rebrand to his POA, we tailored a presentation deck to his strengths and enthusiasm. During our own pitch of our ideas to him, we took note of his body language and responses. If a photograph or mockup we showed made him light up, we included that in his presentation deck so he would communicate that same energy. Anything that fell flat, we left out.

We also gave Geisler a list of questions we anticipated he might be asked, along with our suggested answers. "That was incredibly helpful," says Geisler.

All our preparation equipped Geisler to sell our ideas enthusiastically and well. The homeowners were able to see how we had taken their values and priorities, and integrated them into our concepts. They loved the new brand and signed off on it. Rumbling Bald soon had a new identity.

While it's important to explain your thinking well to your points of contact, that's rarely sufficient. To sell more of your best ideas, prepare your clients to present your concepts just as effectively as you do.

When One Tree Becomes a Grove

Because of the nemawashi-style work we did with Rumbling Bald, Geisler, and his many stakeholders, we built up a lot of trust. The whole community now literally lives in the new brand, and they love it. Anytime newly branded Rumbling Bald merchandise becomes available—golf shirts, T-shirts, etc.—it sells out immediately. The people of Rumbling Bald adore their new identity.

With that first rebrand project, we'd encouraged them to dream, which inspired them to dream even bigger still. And Geisler now knew we'd help him get buy-in on even more audacious ideas.

So, in order to execute on their new brand, and handle ongoing marketing, design, and development work, Rumbling Bald dropped some of their other vendors and put us on retainer. They even asked us to develop a new vacation booking system for them, after an easy approval process with the POA.

What started as a single project became something bigger.

This is because clients are generally thrilled when they find a reliable one-stop shop for many related needs. It simplifies their jobs, and it lets you become a true partner to them, helping them think through strategy rather than simply providing deliverables. "There's a world of difference between the two," says Geisler. "Partnerships are built on trust over time, and they tend to work best when you start small and grow from there."

When you become this partner, helping to shape the client's understanding of the problems they need to solve, you can usually pitch a solution long before anyone else even knows there's something to pitch.

Investing in partnerships like these saves time over trying to sell to new clients. Now, because of the work my company did with Rumbling Bald early, we're in the high-level, ongoing conversations with Geisler. Our finger is on the pulse of what will serve their business and community goals—making it easier for us to present new solutions. Where there's a need my agency can fulfill, the pitch is easy. Their trust in us is already established.

Our business partnership with Rumbling Bald has become something more: a fulfilling relationship of mutual respect that cultivates sustainable abundance for all.

Revisiting Rumbling Bald

Our story continues with Rumbling Bald.

As I write this, we've undertaken a full-scale digital transformation for them—an initiative that emerged from some of our ongoing, high-level conversations with Geisler. It's a bigger investment than their rebrand, with an enormous impact on the community. Geisler might once have worried about getting buy-in for such an ambitious project, but now he doesn't. He knows we're there to help him make the sale, and we know he will sell us well.

Of course, it's not all about selling. In fact, it's mostly not about selling. As this chapter shows, it's also about being a good partner. A good neighbor. We'll tackle that topic in chapter 9.

Chapter 9:

BE A GOOD NEIGHBOR

A Venture Capitalist Who Invests in Relationships

After a career that included stints as a copywriter1 for Walt Disney, a creative director and SVP at a global ad agency, and founder of pioneering digital marketing agency Swirl, Martin Lauber founded 19York, an investment firm with a difference.

19York offers much more than the money Lauber invests. The firm offers relationships: both those Lauber develops as a growth partner to marketing communications and technology firms, and the ones he nurtures among his member agencies.

"The value of those relationships is the most important asset we bring to what is otherwise a transaction," says Lauber. "The money and the back office support are great, but the relationships are key."

Lauber's interest in this unique asset long precedes the founding of 19York. He attributes much of his own personal accomplishments and also Swirl's success to the quality of the connections he has developed with his staff, partners, clients, and community.

As Lauber's example shows, good relationships are important in any career path (and any well-lived life)—but for a small by design company they're even more essential. They define your company and tell your story while providing you with trusted sources of advice and support. They open up new opportunities for you and enhance the satisfaction you'll take in your work.

They are, in fact, among the greatest gifts of staying small by design.

It's Lonely at the Top of Mount Small

In the prelude, I mentioned my brief stint at a large, international communications firm. I'm glad I didn't stay stuck in that narrowing corridor toward the corner office, but I know there would have been certain benefits to walking that path.

For instance, I would have had built-in systems for seeking guidance and mentorship. I would have had cubicle colleagues, then hallway neighbors, division associates, and other office friends as I advanced. We would have all bonded at company events, lunch-hour outings, and the occasional happy hour after work. It would have been an insular existence—my social universe dominated by the people my employer chose to hire—but work companionship would have been there for the taking.

As the founder of a small by design company, I have to put much more effort into building those relationships.

While I have close connections with my employees, there are only a few of them, and half live in other time zones. I also don't have a business partner (sometimes valuable in small by design companies, if you get along very well), so there's no one in my company I can turn to for mentorship or advice on running my business.

In short, it can get lonely at the top of Mount Small.

But it doesn't have to. While it may require more initiative on your part, running a small by design company actually opens up more opportunities to build diverse and meaningful relationships than you would find on a more conventional career path.

It allows you time and space to get to know other business owners and leaders, whether they're clients, partners, contractors, or simply other founders looking to connect. Through the intimate nature of your work, you can build relationships with innovators and visionaries, educators and entrepreneurs, and interesting leaders of culture and commerce wherever you may find them.

When we're small by design, we're primed to better share our stories and struggles, our worries and dreams. We can give and receive advice, support one another through the hard times, laugh about our foibles, and celebrate our victories —more freely than we could in the narrowing corridors of corporate culture.

Small by design opens so many doors to fulfilling relationships that will help you survive the hard times and will make the good times so much better. I hope you'll walk through them often.

The Cup and the Bowl

I haven't yet used the word "network" in this chapter, and I'll include it for the first time here only to say that "networking" is not what I mean when I talk about building good relationships.

Networking has its place in your small by design business strategy, of course. But I'm not a fan of those forced events that are thinly veiled excuses to exchange business cards with people who you hope will turn into clients. Instead, much as Margot Eddy advised in chapter 5, your networking should come from a place of genuine interest and curiosity.

One way I "network" is by regularly attending conferences, industry events, and talks where I know I'll meet like-minded people who may impact my business. I also frequent my favorite coffee shops and my local Creative Mornings series of breakfast talks for creative professionals. I reach out on LinkedIn to people I find interesting. I volunteer on nonprofit boards. I introduce people I'm connected with to one another, and, when there's someone I want to meet, I ask the right people I already know to do the same for me.

Meeting people in this way will help you cultivate a network of useful business connections, a small percentage of which may later develop into genuine relationships, which (as we discuss in chapter 8) are something much more precious.

Lauber told me a story that illustrates the difference.

"I was a young kid, maybe 12 years old, at a restaurant with my family," he says, "and I wanted to order the soup of the day. My mom knew I wasn't going to like the soup—it was clam chowder—but I was insistent. I ordered the soup, and the server asked me if I wanted a cup or a bowl."

"Just get a cup," his mom told him, certain he would never finish it. But Lauber argued with her, determined to get the bowl.

The server intervened, suggesting, "You should get the cup, because a cup is small, but it's deep. A bowl is wide, but it's shallow."

Lauber doesn't know if the server intended anything other than a peaceful resolution to a young boy's tantrum[13], but on the drive home later, his dad used the comparison to illustrate something even bigger. "It's better to go deeper with fewer people," he said. "Be in a cup with

---

13   And he didn't say whether he finished the soup.

those people. Fewer of them will fit, but you can go deeper rather than have a bowlful of relationships that don't go very far."

I'll address other differences between networks and relationships later in this chapter, but depth is an important distinction between them. Networks tend to be wide and shallow, but, like Lauber's dad suggested, I believe you'll get a lot more out of going deep with few.

So don't worry if you don't have hundreds (or even dozens) of movers and shakers in your contact list. Small by design success doesn't depend on a quantity of connections. It's the depth of your relationships that counts.

If You Want to Make It, Don't Fake It: The Value of Vulnerability

Relationships become most meaningful when you do the opposite of what business leaders are often told to do. Don't "fake it 'til you make it." Instead, have the courage to be open and honest.

"My most important relationships have started or cemented when I've dropped the facade of 'I've got this,'" says Lauber. "Meaningful relationships begin or hit a peak when both parties are vulnerable."

This has been my experience too. The bonds that matter most to me —both in business and in life—became so valuable because I've been willing and able to share my struggles and uncertainties, my worries and doubts. Shared my starry-eyed dreams too—the grand ambitions I wasn't sure it was OK to have. They deepened further when I was willing to ask for help, making an implicit admission that I couldn't do everything on my own.

"It's about being completely honest with people," says Lauber, "even when it's not good news. I've come into conversations as an employer talking with an employee and left as peers, because I was vulnerable with them."

The relationships you build through honesty and authenticity will serve you well in both good times and bad. The strength of a relationship may make it worth it for key people to stay with you when you're struggling to make the business work. And when you have a big victory—landing a massive new account, exiting on an acquisition —it will make the celebration all the sweeter as you share both the news and the well-earned rewards with that person.

When you find the strength to be open and honest with people, you provide them with the information they need to give you better support and advice. As you allow others to know you authentically, they're empowered to personalize their guidance to your values, ambitions, and character. It saves time and energy, too.

"Some of the most important and rewarding relationships that I have are with former clients and former business partners," says Lauber, "two groups that conventional wisdom tells you, you're supposed to just write off and forget. For me, it's been very different. Because they know me well, they don't have to ask me a lot of questions. They understand the totality of the questions I ask them and answer with a lot more perspective. They just know me better, so the quality of the support or advice is better too. Those relationships are so valuable to me."

Such relationships can also be critical at key inflection points in your company's growth. When you're vying to level up to a higher impact project or client, you may not have much of a track record to prove you can handle it. So you need someone to believe in you— someone to trust in you and take a chance.

Nothing builds that trust like vulnerability.

Sweet Satisfactions With No Transactions

Even in business, the best relationships are not transactional. If you're connecting with someone only because of what they might do for you,

you're not building a good relationship. If you're constantly checking the balance sheet of what has been given and received, that's not a good one either. Instead, you're simply networking.

"The main difference between networking and relationships is the actions you're willing to take without expecting to gain any sort of immediate reward," Lauber explains. "Keeping score is the worst thing you can do if you're interested in relationships. You have to have faith in the fact that the person values you, that you each will reciprocate when you can."

It's common in a relationship for one person to be able to do more for the other at times. As a business leader, you may often find yourself the person with greater capacity. But the value of relationships goes far beyond give and receive.

While I'll leave out the details to protect the privacy of the employee, to illustrate this, Lauber shared with me a story of a time when an employee was going through a very difficult time. For more than a year, Lauber and his team rallied behind him, making personal and business sacrifices to help him make it through.

With this help, the employee got through the hard time, but within a month he quit the company and went to a competitor. The hours and efforts everyone had given would never be repaid.

Lauber didn't mind at all. "We were happy he was well and his career continued to develop," he says. "We were proud of ourselves for doing the right thing. If we had worried about what we would get in return, we would've cheated ourselves out of the benefit of supporting that person."

Rather than being about transactional benefits, relationships are how you and your company say, "This is who we are." They are the manifestation of your values, providing the gift of your company's story.

I too find great satisfaction in helping people, and my business rewards me by allowing me to help and connect with others in ways I otherwise could not.

For example, I have one friend who is a new mom. Her agency was making around $300,000 in revenue per year, with about six employees. Even before she had her baby, she was always exhausted. It was only getting worse as she juggled running her business and raising her newborn.

I had another friend who was looking to buy a small agency. So I talked up the new mom, connected them together, and got the conversation started. Then I got out of the way.

As a result, they made a deal, and my new-mom friend is now part of a larger organization with the resources to give her a more balanced work life. She recently sent me a happy photo of her and her baby on the beach, along with a message: "I haven't done this in so long."

I had no financial interest in that transaction and didn't make a dime off of it. But that's not what it was about. It was about the joy and satisfaction of being able to help two friends by bringing them together and facilitating a solution to both of their problems.

Whether with your clients and partners, colleagues and contractors, employees, or members of your community, try always to be a good neighbor in similar ways. You'll be reinforcing the power of small by connecting with a level of kindness and care simply not feasible at large companies.

It will probably help your company succeed, but the value of good relationships vastly exceeds anything you'll enter on your P&L report. Good relationships simply make for a better life.

Here are some of the ways you can nurture them.

A ~~Playbook~~ Playground for Being a Good Neighbor

Make Relationships Your Favorite Part of Doing Your Work

When you run a small by design business, it's easy to get hyper-focused on selling and delivering client work. Building and nurturing relationships may seem less urgent—even a distraction from the work you think you're supposed to be doing to help your business grow. Viewed that way, it's no wonder if you never make time for it.

But building those relationships really is part of your job as the leader of a small by design company. To do it well, find a way to make it your favorite part of the job. (It really is mine.)

"I'm notorious for eating lunch at my desk," says Lauber. "But I now force myself to step away more often and go have lunch with someone. I always love it once I'm there."

Relationships also don't have to be separate from doing the work.

"Integrate making and nurturing relationships into the work itself," says Lauber. "Get to know the five, fifteen, or fifty people you work with."

While it may feel counterintuitive when you're busy and short on available time, I find that going deeper in my business relationships is far more satisfying than superficial "connecting." I try to have a clear "why" that motivates every meeting. Not a transactional ambition, but rather a sense of human purpose or genuine curiosity that transforms a networking obligation into a meaningful exchange.

One of the small business owners I mentor started out by texting me occasionally or calling me with a firehose of questions. It was a reactive relationship in which I responded to his questions by dispensing my advice, without any real understanding of his vision for the future. Mentoring him in this way didn't demand a lot of my time or energy, but it also left me without a strong sense of purpose or intention.

So I doubled down on the relationship. I asked him to tell me his story, including the one he wants to tell through his business. With a clearer understanding of his ambitions, I've become more invested in helping him achieve them, and I can bring to him the questions he doesn't yet know to ask. We scheduled a standing monthly call, and in each one I give him action items to complete before the next. Together, we're creating the story of his business while building a stronger relationship too. And that's far more fulfilling.

You don't have to be helping someone (or asking for help) to build a deeper relationship through your work. Simple curiosity can also be your "why," as long as it's authentic.

My agency has worked with several franchise restaurant chains, and I'm genuinely interested in how such a business—so different from my own—runs their operations. A sliver of that knowledge may help me design better digital brand experiences for my client, but I wanted to learn much more than I actually need to know.

Motivated in part by that curiosity, I once flew my team out to Houston, where one franchise restaurant client is based. We took the VP of marketing and others from the executive team out to a fancy dinner. I thought it would give me an opportunity to ask him some questions and learn more about his work.

I was wrong. With eight people around the table at a noisy restaurant, I couldn't have the kind of conversation I'd wanted to have. We made a good appearance and impression. Spent some money on our client. Treated them right. But as a strategy for cultivating a more meaningful relationship with the VP? A complete failure.

When I got back to Atlanta, I emailed the VP and told him about my interest. We scheduled a video call—orders of magnitude simpler and less expensive than the dinner—and we spent an hour in which he talked shop about his work and answered some of my questions.

The education he gave me was fascinating, and I believe he enjoyed having such an enthusiastic listener. That conversation did more to strengthen our relationship than the fanciest dinner ever could.

So don't treat building business relationships like a chore. Instead, find the questions or the genuine connections that motivate you to step away from your desk and engage with all the interesting people in your small by design world.

Be Generous

How do you balance generosity with protecting your business interests? You don't. It's a false dichotomy. Generosity is a powerful driver of business success.

"In today's business world," says Lauber, "being generous is … one of the reasons good people will come to work with you, and one of the reasons people will do business with you."

As with relationships in general, generosity is not something you can analyze on a spreadsheet. For me it's a matter of both faith and experience that generosity brings more abundance to everyone involved.

In the early days of my agency, I hired a full-time photographer. In retrospect, it was a mistake for both of us. Not because he wasn't qualified—he's incredibly talented and did amazing work for my clients. It just turned out that my business model didn't really support the ongoing expense of a staff photographer. (I wish I'd had chapter 6 to read back then, cautioning me about this lack of elasticity.) It was also holding back his career, limiting his ability to take on outside projects that would help him grow his reputation and open up bigger opportunities.

I had to let him go. It was a hard conversation for both of us, but I told him I was confident he'd be more successful as a contractor than he ever would be working full-time for me. Then I told him to hold onto all the photography gear my company had purchased for his use, told him he could work off the cost of it over time as my go-to contract photographer.

I continued to mentor him as he built his own business, fully equipped with high-end lenses, lighting, and all the other gear he needed to establish himself as an in-demand photographer. As I predicted, he's now more successful than he ever would have been as my staff photographer. My agency still has access to one of the best photographers in the business, when we need him, and without the overhead when we don't. And our relationship is stronger than ever.

There are limits to how much I'm able to give —I won't bankrupt my company or sacrifice the quality of the work we do for our clients—but, within healthy boundaries, I try to help as much as I can. It feels good to help people, and I know it has helped my business grow.

So be as generous as you can. It's good for business, and even better for you.

Don't Forget the Smaller Guy

Your company is small, but you're likely not the smallest in your field. You may, for example, partner with even smaller companies and rely on solopreneurs for contract work. I go into this in greater detail in chapter 6, but I bring it up again here because it's important to build good relationships (and be generous) with all those smaller partners you depend on to serve your clients well.

I rely heavily on a digital marketing consultant for many of my clients' digital marketing campaigns. He's a contractor, though he has shared with me that about half of his work is currently with my agency. He's a smart guy, really good at what he does, and I've learned a lot about digital marketing through developing a relationship with him. His consultancy is doing well and growing quickly, and he published a book about digital fundraising for nonprofits.

But recently, he was at that stage of growth where he was always busy, always trying to keep up with all the present work and the many opportunities for growth. He was often overwhelmed.

I well-remembered that time in my own agency's growth, so I asked my virtual assistant (more on her below) to find him his own virtual assistant. She ran the whole search, vetted the candidates, and helped him hire and onboard the person who became his first employee. He was so grateful, and he was able to refocus his energy on the work that mattered most while restoring some health and balance to his life.

Mentoring is another way to extend a hand to those "smaller" than you. I enjoy mentoring people earlier in their careers than me— those who want to follow paths similar to mine. (I've shared some of their stories earlier in this chapter and throughout this book.) I don't do this to ensure some kind of transactional payoff, because, at least for now, the people I mentor are not well positioned to directly contribute to my company's revenue.

But even if my mentees were fiscally flush, that wouldn't be why I'd coach them. Mentoring people deepens and clarifies my own ideas. Their questions force me to examine my own assumptions, sometimes prompting me to change my thinking, or other times helping me articulate something I was doing mostly by instinct.

Many of my mentees' questions prompted advice you've found in this book.

Get to Know People Who Are Very Different From Yourself

"Success begets isolation," says Lauber. "The more successful you get, the less you do things you don't have to do."

Similarly, success can beget homogeneity in your relationships—a tendency to spend most of your time with people very much like yourself.

Resist this drift toward isolation and familiarity. Relationships with people very different from you will make for a better business and a better you too.

"I've known Tasha McVeigh for 30+ years," says Lauber, "since we worked at an ad agency together. I asked her to quit and join mine, and we've built all kinds of things together."

Their collaborations have been so valuable to Lauber because they are not alike.

"We could not be more different," he says. "I'm obnoxious and pushy and impatient sometimes. She's the exact opposite." Those contrasts have taught Lauber greater patience and deepened his empathy, and together they each bring out the best in the other. "Without her, I would certainly not be in a position to be talking to you about relationships."

Similarly, my business has benefited greatly from many relationships I have with people not very much like me.

My virtual assistant, for example, lives on the other side of the world from me, in the Philippines. From her first day working for my agency, she was fast and adept at preparing agendas, scheduling meetings, sending out recaps, and other administrative tasks... all with meticulous attention to detail.

This alone has been so valuable to me and my team. Running an agency in a creative industry, many of the people I work with are, like me, focused on big ideas and generative concepts. Our work is relational, exploratory, and, at least at the beginning, often not well defined.

But the execution of those ideas requires a steadfast dedication to defining and completing every step along the way. With my virtual assistant not only handling but anticipating so much of this for me, I can stay focused on the strategic thinking that I do best, confident that she is not only managing the details, but doing so more thoroughly than I could myself.

In time, we came to know each other better. She told me about the sister she was paying to put through school, the grandmother whose medical care she was providing. She shared her favorite music with me too, by musicians I'd never heard of before. I told her about my vision for my company's future, and shared some of my favorite musicians too. Through this sharing, I became more invested in her career and her family, and she became more engaged in my agency's growth. In other words, across our significant cultural differences and several thousand miles, we built a real relationship.

And through that relationship, I came to see in her the capacity to do much more. The precision she brings to solving complex problems is truly extraordinary, so I asked her to focus her acute attention to detail on larger challenges that move my agency forward, toward my vision for the future. She embraced this challenge with enthusiasm and has since become a critical member of my team—a key contributor to our success.

Even as you become more successful, it's important to keep yourself open to relationships with people unlike yourself. Your business will be better for it, and your life will be richer too.

Building a Neighborhood at 19York

Lauber is now in the process of building a community of good neighbors at 19York, and he has come to use relationship potential as his litmus test of whether to invest in a new company.

"If they value relationships and I get a sense that I want to get to know this person, then the deal becomes secondary," he says. "We invest cash into these businesses, but if that's the reason they want us, they're missing the point. If I have to convince them that the relationship is more valuable than the money, then they're not the right person for us."

As I said earlier in this chapter, these valuable relationships are not just between the member agencies and Lauber. The relationships among the agencies are just as important. 19York is a many-to-many relationship platform of agencies with complementary areas of expertise.

And amidst these interconnected relationships, they share stories, support one another, lift each other up, and shoulder setbacks, so that all can perform at their best and better enjoy their work too.

As Lauber's example shows, a good neighborhood is more than a place for building your material prosperity. It's a place where people come together in love and friendship, supporting each other in happy times and hard, creating a more beautiful life for all.

The best way to build a good neighborhood is to be a good neighbor. Don't bother calculating the ROI on those relationships. Benefits will surely flow to your business, even if they're not easily measured in a pie graph. Far more importantly though, they'll help you live a more fulfilling life.

And that's the best reason of all to stay small by design.

CONCLUSION

The False Fears of Failure

'm often asked about the risks of owning my own company. The question is usually accompanied by some fatalistic statistic about the percentage of small businesses that fail in their first few years. As a new father and responsible husband, don't I worry about the uncertainties of working for myself? Wouldn't I feel more secure with a career at a large, well-established firm?

Quite the contrary.

For all the reasons I've discussed in this book (and more), owning a small by design business doesn't feel like a risk to me. I consider it the most responsible choice for me and my family. As others have written before me, those statistics on small business failure are problematic because they typically lump in owners retiring or exploring new opportunities with all the other reasons a small business might close[14].

Honestly, I'm nowhere near retiring, and my agency is the opportunity I most want to grow. But it's not quibbling over statistical methodologies that eases my mind.

Visibility and Versatility

First, as the owner of a small by design business, I have complete visibility into every aspect of my company's health: the state of current projects, the pipeline of upcoming contracts and prospects, revenue and profitability, and so much more.

I can see, in real time, how well my company is doing. I don't have to wonder or guess about our status based on a semi-annual town hall or board meeting carefully curated by someone else. I constantly know what's working and what's not—what needs my time and attention, or a creative new solution. A large employer would never give me that level of transparency, short of a C-suite position.

Knowledge is a great antidote to anxiety.

When that knowledge tells me that my company needs to adapt to an unexpected challenge or a new opportunity, I don't have to negotiate through layers of internal politics to respond. After a quick conversation with my entire (small) team, I can make a decision to do whatever must be done. I have the ability to pivot quickly and adapt my company while staying true to my values.

Being small by design gives me the visibility I need to be versatile and vigilant in the face of change.

---

14   The True Failure Rate of Small Businesses," Timothy Carter, *Entrepreneur*, January 3, 2021. Retrieved October 14, 2021 from https://www.entrepreneur.com/article/361350

A Job You'll Never Lose

My agency, like any business, feels the impact of major crises and economic recessions. But when calamity strikes, I have layers of stability built in to protect my interests.

When the COVID-19 pandemic sparked a recession in 2020, I did have to lay off some of my more junior employees (giving each a severance package), but I myself didn't go out and start looking for another job.

Instead, I leaned more heavily on seasoned contractors, who were glad to get the work. I doubled down on my leadership team, elevating one to take on creative direction for the company. That freed me to invest more time and energy into evolving the business for resilience during the crisis, restructuring our systems, rethinking our service offerings, and future-proofing the company against the next downturn.

I completed all this restructuring within a few days of the WHO and CDC first declaring COVID-19 a pandemic.

That move was enough for us to not only survive but grow our revenue during the worst public health crisis in a century.

If it hadn't been enough, I could have outsourced less to contractors, further reduced my leadership team, and returned to personally doing much of the work I'd done (and enjoyed) when I was a solo entrepreneur.

I might have been the last employee standing, but I would still have been employed.

As the owner of a small by design business, I will never come into work and leave with all my things packed in a cardboard box. When I show up each day, I have a job.

How many employees of large corporations can say that?

An Investment in Yourself

When you work for a large company, you invest your time and talent in growing the value of the company that employs you. You serve its mission and work toward its vision, pushing your own ambitions to the dusty corners of your life. If you're laid off or quit, you leave behind all that value you generated for them.

As the owner of a small by design business, I've invested years into building something I truly believe in—my company, and myself—and it's now paying dividends, both emotionally and financially. No one can ever take that away from me.

What large employer could ever offer the same?

Work That's Worth It

As I've tried to make clear throughout this book, the benefits of a small by design business don't flow to you automatically just because your company is small. While you can have an outsized impact on your clients and cultivate abundance for yourself and your team, you have to design it right.

This means you have to design for sustainability. Take small off the table by demonstrating to your clients that you can deliver. Build the foundations of flexibility with well-developed systems that allow you to execute quality work reliably, efficiently, and on time. Develop sustainable financial abundance by streamlining your sales and developing long-term relationships with clients whose values align with your own.

You also have to design for impact. Decide on the story you want to tell through your work, then seek out the people and opportunities who will help you tell it well. Share your best thinking with your colleagues, clients, and community, establishing yourself as a trusted leader in your field. Assemble your network of contractors into a team that empowers you to scale to larger projects.

Design for relationships, too. Curate your yeses and nos to nurture the long-term connections that will serve your success. Enlist your clients as ambassadors of your best ideas. Develop and deepen meaningful connections with clients, partners, employees, contractors, and other entrepreneurs.

I'm not suggesting any of this is easy. It's hard work sometimes, though no harder (just different) than a corporate job.

But it's worth it.

From a Narrowing Corridor to an Ever-Widening Way

The fear that gripped me in my first job out of business school was not that I couldn't advance my way down the corridor to that large, windowed, corner office. I was terrified that I could—and would.

In the halls of that massive company, a possible future was laid out before me—every step preordained if I just stayed on the corporate carpeting rolled out so clearly ahead. I only had to sacrifice my own vision, so I could serve the mission handed down to me by the C-suite. I only had to suppress my own values, so I could conform to the culture of my employer. I only had to give up dreaming big and accept the seductive assurances of a predictable path.

That's what large employers really offer: not stability, but predictability. You go in every day knowing what to expect, and knowing the timeline of your advancement, until and unless you show up one morning to find a pink slip and an empty cardboard box waiting at your desk.

Small by design offers a more honest security: not an assurance that nothing will change, but rather that you'll see change coming and have the agency to meet it on your own terms.

The Variant of Me

Sometimes I can't help but wonder what life would have been like if I had indeed walked that well-traveled road offered by my employer.

I'd likely have a VP role by now. I would have forged great connections and found mentors within the large companies I worked with. And I would have made a comfortable living with plenty of predictability within my job.

But I also would never have seen myself at my fullest potential. I never would have learned what I am wholly capable of. Whenever I think about that alternate timeline, I see a diminished version of myself, operating at 50%. I feel so much compassion and sympathy for him.

I discussed this recently with a dear friend of mine, Eric Goldstein, a design agency owner whom I greatly admire. In the 30 years of his career so far, he has spent a total of 18 months working for someone else. During that time he served his employer well, did his job, and took care of their clients to the best of his ability. But he knew the position was preventing him from doing his best work.

"Working for someone else, I never knew what 100% was for me," he told me. "You never realize your own full potential until you work for yourself, and once I saw that I could never go back."

Like Goldstein, I'm so glad I've had the opportunity to discover the fulness of what I can do. I would never choose to trade places with my variant.

The Endless Sky

I have a vision for where my company is headed in the years ahead, but it's an ever-widening way, with so many opportunities to explore, so much to learn, and new adventures every day.

As a small by design business owner, I'm not driving down a smoothly paved road, dutifully following the map and maybe upgrading every few years to a nicer car. Instead, I'm building the road as I go. I can't see my final destination. Who knows where and how far it might take me?

But I wouldn't want it any other way. With joy and wonder, I marvel at the endless sky.

I hope what I've shared here can help you do the same.

ACKNOWLEDGMENTS

Thank you to everyone that made this book a reality. I couldn't have done it without you.

Thank you to Rootstock, my thought leadership team, for giving me the inspiration, energy, and courage to write my first book. Thank you to Rootstock's amazing co-founder and writer, Tom Bell, who helped me define my voice and bring this book to life. Our weekly "Book Friday" meetings will always be a life highlight for me. Thank you to Rootstock's co-founder, Ryan Klee, for always cheering me on and finding ways for me to grow within my community. And thank you to Rootstock's editor, Terra McVoy, for keeping me organized and inspired (and always smiling), throughout this entire process.

Thank you to Reshma Shah, my favorite professor at Emory's Goizueta Business School. Reshma sparked my love both for marketing and leading a team. She has been the wind in my sails throughout my professional career and helped set me on the trajectory I am on today. I would have not been where I am today without her endless support.

Thank you to all my inspiring contributors for sharing their amazing stories in this book. In no particular order, Neil Bedwell, Ron Perry, Steve Clemons, Zach Krame, Cliff Corr, Margot Eddy, Peter Baron, Brad White, Jeff Geisler, Jamie Turner, Michelle Waymire, Sarah Linebaugh, and Martin Lauber.

Thank you to my brilliant friend and mentor, Andrew Jones, for being my sounding board along the way of writing this book. Your boundless wisdom and advice in both my business and book-writing continue to be a driving force in my career.

To my EO Forum, Salt & Light, for your guidance and inspiration in my professional journey. To James Watson, my dear friend and fellow entrepreneur, for supporting me in my entrepreneurial journey from day one. To the brother I never had, Dima Perkis, for always dreaming big with me and being my biggest fan from our early days in business school to present. To ATL Collective co-founder, Micah Dalton, for always kindling my creative spirit.

Thank you to 3 Owl's Creative Director, Brandon Malcolm, for always being by my side and helping me build the beautiful company we run together today.

And thank you to my publisher, Morgan James, and their incredible team of David Hancock, Gayle West and countless others who worked to bring this book to life.

It's an honor to be able to thank all of you and the impact you have made on me. This book would have not been possible with you.

ABOUT THE AUTHOR

David Feldman is the founder of 3 Owl, an award-winning creative agency that crafts nimble brand identities and elegant digital experiences to equip clients for success. With a small core team and a carefully curated network of seasoned contractors, 3 Owl has generated tens of millions of dollars in added revenue for Fortune 500 and small business clients, transformed communities, and helped address the largest public health crisis in a century.

In addition to being a regular writer for Forbes, Feldman is a regular presenter at industry-leading events, and a popular guest lecturer in marketing at Emory University's Goizueta Business School, where he earned a unique dual degree in music and business. He currently resides in Atlanta, GA.

A free ebook edition is available with the purchase of this book.

To claim your free ebook edition:

1. Visit MorganJamesBOGO.com
2. Sign your name CLEARLY in the space
3. Complete the form and submit a photo of the entire copyright page
4. You or your friend can download the ebook to your preferred device

A **FREE** ebook edition is available for you or a friend with the purchase of this print book.

CLEARLY SIGN YOUR NAME ABOVE

Instructions to claim your free ebook edition:
1. Visit MorganJamesBOGO.com
2. Sign your name CLEARLY in the space above
3. Complete the form and submit a photo of this entire page
4. You or your friend can download the ebook to your preferred device

Print & Digital Together Forever.

Snap a photo   Free ebook   Read anywhere

CPSIA information can be obtained
at www.ICGtesting.com
Printed in the USA
JSHW022301140622
27077JS00001BA/2